AF685826

The Jeanine Machine

THE BOOK THAT JEANINE PIRRO DOES NOT WANT YOU TO READ

TO: CARA,

I HOPE YOU DIDN'T FIND THE CONTENT TOO DISTURBING. MY MISSION IS TO BRING DOWN MRS. PIRRO'S WALL OF SECRACY, EVEN IF I MUST DO IT A BRICK AT A TIME!

BEST WISHES,

Richard

11/13/02

The Jeanine Machine

S. RICHARD BLASSBERG

HUDSON HOUSE

The opinions and facts expressed in this publication reflect those of the author. The publisher makes no warranty regarding the contents, facts and opinions, which appear in this publication. The author is the sole legal proprietor and owner of the manuscript. Furthermore the author states that the manuscript is original and that it contains nothing libelous or illegal, in violation of any right of privacy or otherwise in contravention of law, and that any material in the manuscript not created by author is in the public domain, or that the author has obtained written permission to reprint this material in this publication or that use of said material constitutes fair use under current copyright law. The author states that the manuscript, which has been used to produce this publication, does not in any way violate copyright or common law right.
Hudson House is an imprint of Vivisphere Publishing, 2 Neptune Road, Poughkeepsie, New York.

Cover design by Jay Cookingham

Copyright © 2002 by S. Richard Blassberg

ALL RIGHTS RESERVED
Hudson House Imprint
Vivisphere Publishing
2 Neptune Road
Poughkeepsie, NY 12601
800-724-1100

Manufactured in the United States of America
Library of Congress Control Number: 2002113255
Blassberg, S. Richard
The Jeanine Machine
ISBN: 1-58776-141-6

VIVISPHERE PUBLISHING

Table Of Contents

"The only thing necessary for
the triumph of evil is for
good men to do nothing."

— Edmond Burke

Dedication

To

The Hawks

~ PREFACE ~

I come to the task of producing this manuscript with several objectives, the most compelling of which is to expose finally to the full light of public scrutiny the oppressive, malicious, and criminal regime that is the Jeanine Machine. As the Campaign Director for Tony Castro, the most recent challenger to the throne of Westchester District Attorney Jeanine Pirro, I am at once very likely the most knowledgeable and most motivated individual potentially capable of exposing and defining the reign of terror and corruption that is her office. Given the pervasiveness of the evil and depth of the corruption, coupled with the complicity of the print and broadcast media, this testament is truly my profound public duty.

Jeanine Pirro is a great actress capable of playing the victim on a moment's notice. But, more significantly, she possesses a "special mentality," capable of balancing a personal life as the wife and co-conspirator of one of Westchester's more outrageous white collar criminals, and a professional life as the chief law enforcement officer of the same county. She is quite thin-skinned and given to violent and often vulgar outbursts at the mere hint of a challenge to her authority. What makes her situation unique, even amongst corrupt political figures, is the fact that she is not just any office holder, but the chief law enforcement officer of the jurisdiction, with the power to prosecute the innocent and protect the guilty – and she does!

Jeanine Pirro stands for everything undesirable in government, ruling by fear and intimidation. She does not come to her office with clean hands. She does not come with any desire to be a caring public servant. She is a pariah cloaked in the trappings and the power of a tyrant, who preys upon the greed, the lust, and the immorality in others, so resonant within her self.

Every word of this account is documented and true. There is no character assassination, no attempt to sensationalize, because the truth is appalling and shocking enough without enhancement. This book is, after all, about a District Attorney - the highest ranking law enforcement officer in one of the nation's wealthiest, and presumably more savvy counties, Westchester, New York - who is, in fact, an unindicted co-conspirator in a ten year federal income tax fraud.[1] Only in Westchester should it be necessary to say any more. But, as it happens, the tax fraud is just the "tip of the iceberg."

||| One |||

No Good Deed Goes Unpunished

On the morning of April 8, 2000, in the city of White Plains, NY, at 4:25AM, Lee Holt emerged from his apartment building in the downtown section of the city, heading on foot to his job at the Bellantoni Italian Bakery, more than a mile away. It was Sunday and Lee worked most Sundays at the bakery cleaning ovens, sweeping floors, moving sacks of flour and doing whatever general labor his employers might need of him, just as he had been doing six days a week for the past five years.

It was still quite dark as he crossed Mamaroneck Avenue approaching the corner of Martine, a major intersection in the low-rent, commercial district of the city. As he reached the curb, he heard the unmistakable sound of glass breaking from a point about one hundred feet behind him. He next did what few people in his situation would have done, and discovered the truth of the axiom, "*No good deed goes unpunished.*"

Fewer than ten minutes had elapsed since he had stepped out of his building as he now found himself face to face with a burglar who had kicked in the glass front door of La Mode Beauty Salon. The burglar, a young Latino, was desperately rifling the cash register in hopes of discovering Monday's opening change. As he quickly turned to run for a public phone to call police, Lee noticed a car with its engine running on the opposite curb, in a lane of traffic where parking is never permitted.

It was now 4:38AM as Lee stood one hundred and fifty feet from the scene of the burglary trying to communicate with the White Plains Police Dispatcher. The dispatcher can not know that the guy on the line, trying so hard to do his duty as a good citizen, is both developmentally disabled and legally blind. "What street are you on?" came the dispatcher's repeated question.

Unable to read the street sign, Lee called out to two men who had just pulled up across from where he stood. They had gotten out of a car marked "Car Service" but with no phone number, a car that only a mildly retarded person would think was a taxi, or anything other than the unmarked police car that it was. The two occupants, with tattooed forearms and baseball caps turned backward, were shining flashlights into the pizza parlor on their side, completely oblivious to the burglary in progress or the getaway car with engine running parked in a traffic lane less than 50 yards away.

Lee called out "What street is this? I can't read the sign." One "cabbie" responded by walking over to him and placing him in handcuffs. The phone was left hanging, the dispatcher's question unanswered. As he was thrown into the back of the car he protested, "What are you doing? The guy is getting away!" And sure enough he was.

It was a piece of bad police work by two young, but seriously biased, plainclothes detectives. It was a simple matter of racial profiling at its worst. A man who not only had the nerve to be W-W-W-B, (walking to work while black,) but the gall to investigate the sound of breaking glass, and to report a crime in progress, was now under arrest and headed for more trouble than any poor bastard deserved.

En route to Police Headquarters, Lee pleaded with his captors to stop at his apartment for his medication. They flatly refused. He suffered two seizures in the first seven hours in police custody, the second so severe he was rushed to the hospital.

As Project Director for a small HUD sponsored Shelter-Plus-Care program,[2] I was also Lee's case manager. I had worked with him for six years and understood that he was so fearful of incarceration he wouldn't so much as spit on the sidewalk. More than seventeen years earlier, he had been imprisoned for burglary. Because of his developmental disability and refusal to accept prison injustices, he served nearly ten years in nine different prisons, a warden's way of dealing with a "difficult case."[3] I was very concerned when I called in for messages about noon, as I did most Sundays, to hear his weak and exasperated voice from the Westchester County Jail.

Advising them that I was a former county probation officer, I learned from jail authorities that he wouldn't be going to court for arraignment until Tuesday. I realized that he might very well not be released at his arraignment, and so I gathered clothing for several days and his medications from his apartment and headed up to the county jail, arriving before 2PM.

It was chilly and very windy as I stood in line with family members of other inmates waiting for 3 o'clock visiting hour. It did not matter that I wouldn't be allowed to see him, but merely to drop off his clothes and medications, I was compelled to wait in line in the cold. I wasn't a P.O. anymore, as I was many years ago, and I carried no badge.

Once inside, the wait was almost as long. I knew that Lee did not belong there, and I felt confident there was some misunderstanding. I thought "I'll see the arresting officers and get to the bottom of this."

Monday morning brought the first chance to speak with Lee. He phoned my office from the jail and explained all that had happened. He had already called the bakery to reassure his employer. He was frightened, very upset, and frustrated.

I contacted Butch, one of his bosses. We agreed to meet at City Court Tuesday morning for the arraignment. He knew Lee well after five years of employment. He, too, had welcomed him into his home and trusted him as I did. He agreed "there must have been some mix-up here." I had reached the Legal Aid Society of Westchester, earlier, and assured Butch that Lee would have legal representation at his arraignment.

Tuesday morning brought disappointment. Butch and I came to court expecting that Lee would plead innocent to the charges and would either be released on his own recognizance or bailed for a nominal sum, which Butch was prepared to deal with. Instead, he was returned to jail because having had a prior conviction, it would be necessary to conduct his bail hearing in County Court on Thursday.[4]

Following the arraignment, Butch and I spoke with his Legal Aid attorney, a Mr. Arthur Doran. Doran and I had spoken at some length on Monday, and he came to court with a pretty complete picture of his client and sufficient reason to accept his innocence. Now, having met and spoken with Lee in the holding pen, he seemed pretty confident in that belief.

As we were about to part company, Doran informed us that he wouldn't be seeing us at the bail hearing on Thursday. Realizing that I would have to re-explain to another attorney all that I had explained to Doran, I inquired as to why he wouldn't be in County Court. What Doran now said opened my eyes to a system which I had serious questions about more than thirty years earlier when I served as a Westchester County Probation Officer.

Doran explained that, in Westchester, Legal Aid attorneys move from court to court and that it was unlikely that a defendant who appeared twice or more in the same court, or who went from one court to another would have the same attorney representing him at every appearance. He further explained that the only time a defendant using Legal Aid would have the services of the same attorney all the way through a case was when he refused to plead out and went to trial. Then, and only then, would the attorney be pulled out of the pool and assigned to work on that case.

The city court building also housed the police headquarters. On the floor above the courtrooms I found the Detective Division and the two plainclothes detectives who had arrested Lee. I spent some forty-five minutes detailing for them what Lee was really all about.

I told them of his desire to do the right thing at all times. I explained how he had introduced seven other of my clients to his employer, and that two were still working at the bakery. I explained that he was on the street at 4:30AM "because that's the time he goes to work every day," and that he was "so fearful of prison he wouldn't dream of committing a crime."

Finally, I explained that when they arrested him he was actually on the phone reporting the burglary to their dispatcher. "Why didn't you check the tape of his 911 call?" I pleaded. They wouldn't give an inch. They couldn't admit that they had made a bad mistake and that their account was a fiction. They were two bad cops, period!

Thursday came and I made a point of arriving at court early, in hopes of speaking with the young woman I was told would be representing Lee. She was sharp, understanding and compassionate. She absorbed all that she needed to know in less than ten minutes, and accurately recited the details to Judge Kenneth Lange. The judge, for his part, saw humor in the situation, as Lee stood before him in "cola bottle" thick eyeglasses. With a smile, he said to the young assistant D.A. who had just demanded $10,000 bail, "You know you don't have a very good case here. You are charging a man who is legally blind with Burglary 3rd as the look-out in a burglary."

As Lee stood expressionless, a sense of relief came over me as the judge said "I'm releasing you on your own recognizance and to the supervision of your case manager." Unfortunately, the good judge's words were wasted on the D.A.'s office, and specifically on Bureau Chief Paul Scharf and his boss, Jeanine Pirro.

Two weeks later we were back in City Court only to discover that the actual perpetrator had been apprehended by the New Rochelle Police because the car he used in the burglary had been stolen there, and that he too was appearing and was also represented by Legal Aid. The Court was now confronted with a situation which was a conflict of representation and which required Judge Joanne Friia to appoint counsel. Normally, 18b Counsel, as they are referred to, are reserved for misdemeanor cases where clients can not afford a private attorney. This case, a felony, was the exception.

The actual perpetrator, a fellow named Miguel Alvarez, came into the courtroom in handcuffs and leg irons and refused to address the judge, even when spoken to directly. He was assigned an attorney named Jeffrey Cohen who accompanied him back to the holding pen to try to talk some sense into him. Lee was assigned another attorney who spoke down to him and took no time to determine the facts of the case, or whether his remarks were fully understood.

As we stood in the corridor of the court, I could see exasperation in Lee's face as this fellow was giving him short shrift.

Walking back to my office he turned to me and said, "If I have to use that lawyer, they may as well lock me up right now!" Lee was scheduled to return to court in two weeks, but there was no way it would be with this lawyer.

I reached Butch at the bakery. He appeared anxious for good news. He asked, "How did it go?" half expecting me to tell him that the whole thing was just a big misunderstanding and that the charges had been dropped. Instead, I shared the problem about the assigned counsel and told him that we needed to find Lee his own lawyer, and needed to figure out how to pay for it. I explained that the next court appearance was two weeks off and asked him to get back to me with any suggestions.

About a week later Lee came to my office with news from Butch. Butch had agreed to lay out one thousand dollars to retain Peter Goodrich, his own lawyer. Lee would pay Butch back from his wages over a period of weeks, possibly months. I reached Butch the following day to thank him for his kindness to Lee and also to learn a little about Mr. Goodrich, a name I didn't think I recognized.

Lee felt better knowing he would have his own attorney, and even a little hopeful that the whole mess would soon be over. We had already been to court three times and nothing encouraging had come from the D.A. He was both worried and indignant that he was being prosecuted not only for something he didn't do, but for reporting the crime! It was hard not to agree with him — and harder yet, to tell him he should have kept walking.

For my part I was angry, first with the officers responsible, and then with the D.A.'s office which surely had the tape of Lee's "911" call and had to know he was innocent. My feelings about the detectives were based upon my own investigation of the scene and the surrounding area the day after the incident as well as my encounter with them at headquarters the following day. Based upon the information Lee had given me from the jail on Monday, the day after the incident, I had a few questions that only a field investigation might answer.

Lee had mentioned that while he was on the phone trying desperately to tell the police dispatcher where he was located and the two plainclothes cops pulled up across the street, they immediately began shining their flashlights on the pizza parlor windows. I wondered what the possible connection was.

As I approached Sunshine Pizza I found no less than four separate broken windows, with low level impact shatters, as though someone had tried unsuccessfully several times to kick in a window and perhaps break in. A picture of what probably had happened emerged. The burglar had, at first, tried to break into the pizzeria, and making several tries, might very well have been spotted either by a passing motorist with a cell phone, or possibly a resident of the apartment building directly across the street. Either way, a phone call might have been made to 911, just minutes before Lee's call, directing police to the pizzeria. This might explain the appearance of the unmarked car as Lee was calling in the beauty salon break-in. Maybe the burglar just kept kicking windows until he broke one and entered.

Oblivious of the action at the beauty salon just 50 yards up the street, as they were arresting an innocent man, and too cocky to even check out his story with their dispatcher, the two cops blew it big-time. Naturally, as the facts came to light, they concocted a total fiction for their arrest report, hoping to cover their collective asses.

I arrived at City Court before Lee, intending to meet with

Mr. Goodrich to fill him in on events so far; all the things he needed to know about his new client. I was seated for a few minutes when Goodrich entered the corridor. We instantly recognized each other from a time more than thirty years earlier when I was a probation officer and he was an assistant D.A. We briefly exchanged personal updates and quickly turned to the case at hand. I was comfortable and confident that Lee would be well represented.

Our conversation centered on the fact that the D.A. certainly had a copy of the 911 tape, and that given that evidence, must surely realize Lee's innocence. "If it's clearly exculpatory, and they have it, why are they continuing to prosecute him?" I asked. Peter shrugged his shoulders and said, "We'll see when we get a copy of it." Fortunately, we were one of the early cases on the calendar. Peter made the necessary motion for transfer of the case from the appointed attorney, received the file, and was given a new date several weeks later.

Walking out of the courtroom, Lee turned to his new attorney and thanked him for taking the case. Peter graciously acknowledged him and assured him that everything would work out okay. As we shook hands he assured me that he would get a copy of the dispatcher's tape, if it existed, along with some other information on a discovery motion he would file within the next few days.

Several weeks would pass before Lee would appear in court, for the fifth time. He was nervous and needed constant reassurance. He wasn't certain if his sister or his aunt really believed him. The whole affair reminded him of a period in his life he really wanted to put behind him: the time he spent in prison when no one came to visit and no one seemed to care if he was alive. He understood that over all those years the lack of visitors and correspondence contributed to the abuse he suffered at the hands of prison guards and officials.

It was now early August, and Mr. Goodrich called to be certain that I would remind Lee that he was due in court the following Tuesday. Almost as an afterthought, as he was about to take another call, he said, "we received a copy of the tape yesterday. I haven't had a chance to listen to it yet."

I arrived later than I had planned at court. I had gotten an urgent message from the landlord of another client that there had been "another incident with Howard and his neighbor," and he was ready to evict Howard. A brief stop at the neighbor's apartment patched things up for the moment.

As I walked into the courtroom, Lee was still seated, waiting to be called. There were an unusually large number of arraignments to be dealt with and it was already approaching 11AM. Lee would likely not be called for another half-hour. Peter had been looking through a file folder in the attorney's section as I entered. He looked up as I sat down next to Lee and motioned to me to step into the corridor.

Peter came out behind me. I could sense the disgust in his voice as he began to relate his earlier conversation with Paul Scharf, the Bureau Chief, who at this point had been prosecuting the case for more than four months. Having received and listened to the tape, Peter had come to court expecting Scharf to be willing to dismiss the charges. "The tape is clear and it corroborates Lee's story," he said flatly.

"So what's the problem?" I asked.

"They want him to plead to a misdemeanor," he snapped.

We reentered the courtroom. As I sat down next to Lee he was looking at me with an expectant expression. I was thinking, "the D.A.'s a bastard," but I whispered "It's all right."

The case was called. Judge Leake, a tough, no-nonsense black woman inquired as to what, if any, progress had been made between the sides, each responding that their positions were unchanged and that they were ready to move forward. The judge set a date for a pretrial hearing.

As the three of us parted company outside the courtroom, we agreed to get together at Peter's office before the next court date. Walking back toward my office, Lee was agitated and very vocal. He was having trouble paying Butch back as quickly as he had hoped.[5] "More court appearances are going to cost even more," he groaned. "I'm not goin' to plead guilty to nothin', no way, no how."

Back at my office I couldn't help commenting to my assistant about the frustration and anger I felt. "Here we have a man, mildly retarded and legally blind, being mercilessly prosecuted by a DA who surely must know he is innocent and is, in fact, the person who reported the crime. Yet this same D.A.'s own husband was convicted on all counts by a federal jury for massive tax fraud just six weeks ago after a trial for which she publicly castigated the United States Attorney for prosecuting him."

In the weeks that followed I couldn't get Lee's circumstances off my mind. Paul Scharf was no low-level assistant D.A.. He was a Bureau Chief and taking his "marching orders" from Jeanine Pirro. In my frustration over my client's situation, I started thinking about Miguel Alvarez, the actual perpetrator. We hadn't seen him since he was assigned Mr. Cohen.

On a hunch, I called Peter Goodrich and asked him to

check into what had happened to him. A few days later Peter came back with the news that "Alvarez had pled out." Instinctively, I asked, "can you get a transcript of his pleading?" I wasn't sure what, if anything, we might find, but I thought, "from Jeanine Pirro's Office, anything is possible."

Several weeks passed before Peter called to say he had the transcripts from Mr. Cohen, and "why don't you come by my office with Lee next Friday so we can discuss things before we appear in court again." I was anxious to see what was in the transcripts and Lee certainly needed to make some decisions before his next appearance.

It was now October and Lee had been to court five times. The whole ordeal was taking a huge emotional and financial toll on him. In trying to pay back his employer for the retainer, he was neglecting other bills. His phone had been turned off. He felt very upset and put out. His family, who at first seemed not to believe him, were now calling me up and running their mouths about going to Al Sharpton for help. It was becoming more than Lee could deal with.

As we entered Peter's office, he could see that things were really beginning to get to Lee. He came toward us, placing his arm on Lee's shoulder as he handed me a copy of the transcript from Alvarez' pleading, almost two months earlier. As I quickly read through it, Peter asked Lee if he had decided what he wanted to do. Before Lee could respond, Peter said, "Look, I know this has been rough on you, and you are free to do what you think is best for you. But if you take a plea, I won't stand next to you."

I had stopped reading as Peter's tone became stern. I looked into Lee's face as he got the message. He needed to go forward, no matter what the risks or cost.

There was a deafening silence as I continued to examine the transcript. Lee said not one word but moved his head from side to side with a tight-lipped expression. Peter broke the silence, "Is that what you were expecting?" I glanced up, "Is there no limit to their cruelty?"

The court transcript revealed that nearly two months earlier, in County Court, as Alvarez stood under oath, pleading guilty to a lesser charge, Assistant D.A. Bernhard, clearly under orders and with the full knowledge of Jeanine Pirro, approached the defendant. "You admit that on April 8, 2000, in the City of White Plains, County of Westchester, State of New York, while being aided, abetted and acting in concert with another person, that you knowingly entered unlawfully into a building with the intent to commit a crime therein?" (Whereupon Mr. Cohen and Alvarez conferred off the record.)

Mr. Cohen: "He says he did it himself. He did not do it with anybody else. That's his statement."

Not satisfied with that answer, Bernhard went further, "Were you present at that location, on April 8th, at the beauty salon?"

Alvarez: "Yes, I was present. I was with nobody else."

Bernhard: "Was Lee Holt with you?"

Alvarez: "No. I told the police then."

Bernhard: "Lee Holt already pleaded guilty to acting in concert. I don't know who he is protecting. It's already a done deal."

As I looked up from the transcript, Goodrich was smiling. In that moment, we both knew that we had found the solution to Lee's problem. His agony would soon be over. If necessary, we would hang the D.A.

Peter Goodrich was a gentleman of an attorney, and, as far as I could tell, not given to wild outbursts or accusations. As outraged as he might have been with what Mrs. Pirro and her office had tried to pull on his client, and armed, as he was, for bear, he walked into court planning to reason once again with Bureau Chief Scharf. He would ask him to dismiss the charges against Lee because Lee was innocent, as evidenced by the tape of the 911 phone call, which clearly corroborated his account of his activities at the time of the burglary, and, because the actual perpetrator had already been disposed of under a plea agreement.

As Lee's case was called, I took up a position close to where Peter and Scharf would confer before each was addressed by Judge Friia. Peter was very controlled and proceeded as he had planned. Paul Scharf was cold and unmoved. He was there to get a conviction, possibly only to a violation, but a conviction nonetheless!

Excusing himself to the court, Peter stepped around the partition and approached me. "He's not willing to be reasonable." "You don't have a choice, - put the transcript in his face," I whispered in anger. With Judge Friia looking on, Peter did precisely that. The prosecutor's face turned ashen as a forced smile came over it.

Before the Judge could solicit a response, Scharf broke the awkward silence. "Your honor, the People move to dismiss the charges against the Defendant, provided he agrees not to civilly prosecute the State of New York, the County of Westchester, or the City of White Plains."[6]

Peter asked the Court for a moment to confer with his client. Lee stepped out of the box to speak with Peter and me. He was relieved and confused at the same time. Peter explained his options and his rights. It was more information than he was prepared to handle. He turned to me, "what do you think I should do?"

His question caught me a little off guard. I had expected we would get a dismissal, armed as we were with the Alvarez transcript. But I never considered the possibility that Scharf would attempt to get Lee to waive his right to sue for malicious prosecution and false arrest, as a condition of granting the dismissal!

I had mixed emotions. On the one hand, I wanted reprisal for what the D.A. had been doing to him for months but, on the other hand, I just wanted to see him free of the whole ugly mess. The words just came to my mouth. "Look, you need to be free of this. You've suffered enough already."

Lee walked out of the court a free man, more than seven months of prosecution, harassment and grief behind him. There was relief but no satisfaction. No one in the courtroom other than Scharf, and the three of us, knew why the charges were dismissed, not even the judge.

There would be no apology, and no acknowledgment from the District Attorney, whose sworn duty it was to protect the innocent, that a grievous mistake had been made. There would be no sense that some terrible wrong had been righted, or even that a truly innocent man would be set free. For all anyone knew, Lee might have been dismissed on a procedural technicality.

I thought to myself, "what if Lee had not had such a caring employer and competent, dedicated lawyer? What if the deceit and maliciousness of the D.A.'s office exposed in the transcript had never been uncovered?" A decent citizen who took the time and the personal risk to observe and report a crime in progress might well have been convicted as a participant.

I could not help the anger and outrage with which I came

away from the whole affair. It was knowing that the D.A. of Westchester County had no problem sending a clearly innocent man to prison, but could vilify the United States Attorney for prosecuting her husband, one of the most outrageous white collar criminals in the county, and her co-conspirator in a massive, ten-year tax fraud. The only satisfaction for me came from the knowledge that, by our wits and our persistent effort, we had foiled a corrupt and jaundiced prosecutor's attempt to convict and incarcerate an innocent and powerless citizen merely to notch one more conviction on her record. And, while it was Paul Scharf who carried out the cruel game, it was Jeanine Pirro who was calling the shots. As any knowledgeable defense attorney knows, every decision, every disposition from her office always comes through her.

It is important to recognize that when Lee appeared in court in October of 2000, the actual perpetrator Miguel Alvarez, had four times denied any involvement by Lee in the April 8, 2000 burglary – once at his arrest, and three times at his pleading to reduced charges. Those four denials constituted significant exculpatory information,[7] which was intentionally withheld by Jeanine Pirro in her cruel attempt to obtain the conviction of a clearly innocent man.

||| Two |||

The Pirro Brothers Circus

In early June of 2000, after many months of motion practice, and several attempts to avoid prosecution for ten years of federal income tax fraud, Albert Pirro, husband of the District Attorney of Westchester County, was finally brought to trial in the Federal Court House in White Plains, together with his brother Anthony, who had prepared his and Jeanine's income tax returns. Simply stated, Al was charged with having filed false personal income tax returns between 1988 and 1997 for the purpose of evading more than one million dollars in taxes. Essentially, the scheme involved the payment of personal expenses with corporate funds so as to enjoy the write-off from corporate taxes without declaring such payments as personal income.

What made the prosecution so worthy of public attention was the fact that not only was the defendant Al Pirro, the husband of D.A. Jeanine Pirro, but also that nine of the ten tax returns in question were filed jointly and signed by her as well, "under penalty of perjury for any knowingly false declaration." She was not indicted, however, for reasons that U.S. Attorney Mary Jo White will probably take to her grave.

Surely, Mrs. Pirro, as an attorney and as the District Attorney of Westchester County, could not reasonably qualify under the terms of the "innocent spouse clause." Given that fact, Mary Jo White could have but one of two reasons for giving Mrs. Pirro a free "stay out of jail pass." Either she did not possess sufficient evidence of her culpability beyond the mere signing of so many years of false returns, or she believed that Jeanine Pirro was so popular that it might have been difficult to get a conviction against Al if she included her. Most observers who closely followed the evidence presented believe that there was more than ample proof of Jeanine's hands-on involvement in the tax fraud to have convicted most any spouse as a co-conspirator.

The events leading up to the trial, as well as the trial itself, were very revealing about the personal lives and the activities of both Al and Jeanine Pirro. These were no *Eleanor and Franklin* but more like *Bonnie and Clyde.* Their true characters were clearly exposed and the image was revolting to say the least. Al, for his part, was such a "stand-up guy" that he attempted to avoid prosecution by blaming all he had done to cheat the Government out of more than million dollars, on his brother. He went so far as to secretly tape record conversations with him for that purpose.

Jeanine, not to be outdone by Al, it was revealed, had lent two of her top criminal investigators to him so that he could avoid making child support payments by discrediting Jessica Marciano, the mother of his seventeen year-old illegitimate daughter. What a women's advocate! What an example!

Considering all that was likely to come out at trial, straight-thinking people would have opted for a nolo-contendre plea. But then, this was Al and Jeanine Pirro, and they were accustomed to getting their way. Rules were for everyone else. D.N.A. testing finally established that Al was indeed the father, after ducking his responsibilities for 16 years.

As the trial approached there was speculation in the media as to whether Jeanine would attend. She soon put that question to rest as she not only showed up, but also gave press statements at the court house castigating and vilifying Mary Jo White for having the nerve to prosecute her husband. One might ask, what reasonable person, similarly situated, would have carried on as Jeanine Pirro did?

Her comments concerning the Government's right to prosecute her husband most clearly betrayed what Jeanine is really all about. Listening to her remarks it was obvious that she feels she and her husband are above the law, and that, in fact, there should be a two-tiered system of law enforcement – one for the Pirro's and their pals, and another for the rest of us! Her unbridled display of anger at the fact that the U.S. Government had the audacity to prosecute her husband and deal with his criminal conduct as it would deal with any other tax cheat, was both unprofessional and reprehensible coming from a prosecutor.

There was, however, a method to her madness. In castigating Mary Jo White, Jeanine repeatedly charged her with politically motivated prosecution intended to derail Jeanine's political career. There were many who believed that were it not for the tax fraud issue, Jeanine would likely have been the Republican candidate for United States Senator opposite Hillary Rodham Clinton. And, while Jeanine might have firmly believed that, still her vilification of the U.S. Attorney had a very specific purpose.

Jeanine was playing to the public, but specifically to the jury who might buy into the notion that the prosecution and trial were a "politically motivated witch hunt," and find Al innocent, given their payback of $1.2 million.[8] Of course, Jeanine was very careful not to betray the fact that she and Al knew about their tax problem as far back as December of 1997. Her fallback strategy, in the event that she failed to influence the jury's verdict favorably, would be to deny any personal involvement, and she has pursued that strategy since Al's conviction on all counts.

The trial produced several thousand pages of testimony,

much of which involved the knowing, hands-on participation of Jeanine Pirro. It is noteworthy that four of the ten fraudulently reported tax returns were filed while she was the District Attorney and three prior ones when she was a County Court Judge. The fact that she continues, since the trial, to simply state that for all of those years, she "did not know what she was signing," is a cruel insult to the intelligence and common sense of the more than 900,000 people of Westchester of whom she sits in judgment every day.

Amongst the many unlawful acts in furtherance of the tax fraud scheme, of which she was not merely plainly aware, but, was in fact, an active co-conspirator and participant, seven instances in particular provide the most compelling and irrefutable evidence of her culpability.

1. The "Sham Car Loan"

The "Sham Car Loan," as the Government entitled it, was described in detail in their opening argument, pages 43 through 46 of the transcript. According to the U.S. Attorney's Office, in 1993 the Pirro's decided to purchase the 1989 Mercedes Benz sports roadster which Mrs. Pirro had been driving as her personal car under a 4-year lease held by the Ferris-Pirro Corporation, later renamed Flagler Corporation. The purchase price of the car, now four years old, was approximately $42,000. Mrs. Pirro had been the exclusive driver of the car, which bore her special judge plates when she sat as a County Court Judge.

To purchase the car, Jeanine went to the Hudson Valley National Bank, carrying a title and registration from Flagler Corporation. She applied for and obtained a personal car loan to cover the full purchase price of the car, using the car, which she did not personally own, as collateral. She immediately deposited the proceeds of that loan into Flagler Corporation, which then made monthly payments against the note and ultimately paid it off. Flagler Corporation, of course, wrote off the purchase of her personal car as a 'business expense' just as it had written off the lease for four years.

This particular scheme, intended to create the illusion of legitimacy, was clearly a "sham" as labeled by federal prosecutors. Jeanine Pirro knew every step of the way what she was doing. She knew that she had applied for the loan. She knew that she placed the proceeds into Flager Corporation. And, she knew that she never paid back one penny of the loan, all for the purpose of allowing one of Al Pirro's corporations to write off the purchase of the car as a business expense.

One might question how it was that a bank would give a loan of more than forty thousand dollars to someone who offered as collateral a car which she did not hold title to. The answer, quite simply, is that the "sham car loan" was just one of several instances in which the Hudson Valley National Bank made sweetheart deals with the Pirros. Bonnie and Clyde had their method of dealing with banks. Jeanine and Al have theirs.

Another case in point; on December 22, 1997, Jeanine and Al Pirro apparently needed to raise a lot of money in a hurry. It is safe to say that they had very likely just been tipped off to their federal income tax liability and were under pressure to pay off nearly two million dollars in evaded taxes and penalties assessed against them. In any event, they arrived at the Hudson Valley National Bank with the deed to their home in Harrison, N.Y., in hand.

Now, the records of the Westchester County Clerk's Office of Land Records reveals that the deed they brought to the bank that morning listed the owners of that property as Jeanine Pirro and Albert Pirro, as joint tenants by the entirety. In the presence of bank officials, and with their full knowledge and consent, Jeanine and Al proceeded to pass title to the property from their joint ownership to ownership by Jeanine alone. Having thus relieved Al Pirro of any right of ownership in the property, Jeanine proceeded to borrow 1.375 million dollars from the bank, personally, offering the deed to her home as mortgage collateral. Interestingly, although Jeanine signed the mortgage, Al signed the promissory note.

Apparently, $1.375 million was not enough to satisfy their liability because Jeanine and Al were back at Hudson Valley Bank just eight days later, on December 30th, to borrow another $.5 million using the same property as collateral, under the same terms and conditions as before. One must ask why a bank would have permitted such a transfer, or likely insisted on it. Quite simply, the Pirros were not only aware of their tax liability, but also of the fact that Al would be held liable in any criminal action to follow – and Jeanine would be spared! In short, the Pirros had cut their deal as early as December of 1997.

During the eighteen months of motion practice, which preceded the trial, the Government held to their position that Al's revision of ten years of income tax returns, combined with the taxes, penalties and interest paid, were tantamount to an admission of guilt. Ordinarily, the Internal Revenue Service may investigate and recover unpaid income taxes for a period of seven years. However, when there is a charge of tax fraud federal regulations permit prosecution and collection as far back as ten years, but not beyond, thus, in effect, creating a ten-year statute of limitations on federal tax fraud. It is entirely conceivable, therefore, that

Jeanine and Al Pirro may have been engaging in fraudulent tax reporting practices long before 1988 but simply could no longer be prosecuted for it.

If it was the Government's strategy to "tip off" the Pirros and then wait for them to react, it was certainly very clever and effective. However, the "sham car loan" was not the only transportation related tax avoidance scheme in which Jeanine Pirro had direct hands-on involvement.

2. <u>Jeanine's personal use of a corporation chauffeur</u>.

The law firm of Pirro and Monsell, one of Al Pirro's many corporations, employed a Mr. Patrick McGillicuddy as a chauffeur for the firm for approximately four years between 1988 and 1992. Mr. McGillicuddy testified at trial that during his tenure he spent approximately half of his time doing work for the Pirro family. Testifying for the Government, McGillicuddy stated that his daily work included driving the Pirro children to school, camp, skating classes, the doctor's office and the grocery store.

When he wasn't chauffeuring the children, he would run errands to the laundry, the drug store and other business establishments. His duties also included trips to the veterinarian with the family pets as well as family trips to the airport or to Jeanine's mother's house in upstate Elmira. He was also involved in transporting Jeanine to political events.

Testimony indicated that Mr. McGillicuddy was no mere company employee, whose services were borrowed by Jeanine for personal and household chores. In fact, he acted as a sort of surrogate grandfather to the Pirro children, and was thoroughly interviewed by Jeanine before being hired by the law firm controlled by Al Pirro. In actuality, Mr. McGillicuddy was employed by Jeanine as a household employee, although he was never paid by her or with personal funds.

Interestingly, not only was Mr. McGillicuddy not paid by Mrs. Pirro for his household services, but he was not paid by the law firm which hired him. Instead, as a part of the elaborate tax fraud scheme practiced by the Pirros, he was paid with corporate checks drawn on Suburban Messenger Corp. and P.M. Messenger Corp.. At trial, Assistant U.S. Attorney Cathy Seibel described those companies as "empty shells with no material assets, having no legitimate business purpose except to further the tax fraud."

As with the sham car loan, there could be no way in which Jeanine Pirro was not an active, knowing, hands-on participant in this aspect of the overall tax fraud scheme. After all, she knew that Mr. McGillicuddy was a household employee, under her control, hired with her approval, and employed at will, but that she paid not one penny of his salary from personal funds. As an attorney and a person of higher than average intelligence and exposure, she most certainly knew that she was a party to, and signatory to, a fraudulent tax scheme. As an Assistant D.A. and as the County Court Judge that she was during the period of Mr. McGillicuddy's employment, she knew that her conduct and her husband's conduct, with regard to this employee, was clearly fraudulent and in violation of the law.

As with the sham car loan and the elaborate transfer of funds between Pirro Corporations to obfuscate and conceal the tax fraud, so too was the intent in the method involved in paying McGillicuddy's salary. The funds to pay him were paid into the P.M. Messenger account by the law firm of Pirro and Monsell, to make it appear that the law firm was paying for legitimate messenger services, when, in fact, it was paying mostly for personal services to the Pirro family. The payments were then deducted as business expenses, and never declared as income by Jeanine or Al on their joint personal tax returns, in obvious and blatant violation of the law.

3. A Mercedes 190 Sedan for Jeanine's Mother

Another transportation related tax fraud by Jeanine and Al involved the gift of a 1992 Mercedes 190 Sedan for Jeanine's mother, Esther A. Ferris of Elmira, New York. Once again the car registration was in a corporate name, Distinctive Properties of Yonkers. Mrs. Ferris was not an employee of that or any other corporation of Al Pirro's.

The cost of the car, the personalized license plate, "100EAF," the service and maintenance, and the insurance were all paid by the corporation and deducted as business expenses, even though Jeanine's mother, Mrs. Ferris, in Elmira, New York, was the exclusive operator of the car. But, the lease and purchase fraud was not limited to Jeanine's and her mother's Mercedes. A secretary of Al's, a Ms. Cain would testify at the trial that over time the Pirro's used the same scheme to finance "a dozen different cars," including a Bentley and a Ferarri.

Despite Jeanine's repeated denials, following Al's conviction on all counts, that she had any knowledge of their joint income tax fraud, it is only reasonable to expect her to have been aware of the source of funds for a gift to her own mother — particularly a gift as substantial as a new Mercedes automobile.

4. Jeanine's "Zoe Baird Problem" with a Pirro Twist.

Very early in the trial the Government introduced the Pirro's "Nanny Tax Problem," as prosecutor Cathy Seibel referred to it. However, before bringing on witnesses, the Government had to answer and overcome a defense motion to "confine the Government to describing the 'Zoe Baird Problem' as just involving the nannies' tax returns," which Ms. Seibel declared was "incorrect." In fact, as prosecutor Seibel would point out, it was important to bring out the fact that not only had the nannies not paid their taxes, but "that it also involved the fact that the Pirro's had not paid the payroll taxes."

The Government wanted to make it crystal clear that there was a 'Zoe Baird Problem.' And, indeed, there was, not only in the fact that the payroll taxes had not been paid by the Pirros as their employers, but more significantly because Jeanine was a prominent political figure, as was Zoe Baird. As Ms. Seibel promised, her witnesses would "testify that the Pirros were deeply concerned about their nanny tax problem and how it might impact the future political career of Mrs. Pirro." From the Government's standpoint it was important to bring out Jeanine's and Al's concerns because it caused them to hire accountants and a political consultant, all of whom were paid with corporate funds, unlawfully deducted as business expenses. And, that, after all, was what the case they were prosecuting against Al and his brother was all about.

With regard to Jeanine, the unindicted co-conspirator, the significance of this aspect of the tax fraud conspiracy is that it puts the lie to her repeated claims that she merely, "left all matters relating to taxes up to Al," and signed all those joint tax returns "without paying attention to what they contained." Better yet, her remark, upon announcing her candidacy for a third term, intended to sound like a mild admission, "I should have paid more attention to my family's finances." Right, Jeanine!

The unique significance of Jeanine's and Al's handling of her 'Zoe Baird Problem' lies in the fact that it clearly points to their brazen and intentional commission of tax fraud, even as they were trying to avoid the consequences of their previous tax fraud as far back as 1991 and 1992. Similarly, it establishes Jeanine's awareness of their fraudulent tax activities, and her hands-on involvement and vital personal stake in the ongoing cycle of fraudulent conduct. It shows the power of greed, and the craving for wealth, even in the face of possibly serious political consequences and criminal prosecution. It shows, without question, that she was a very culpable co-conspirator despite U.S. Attorney Mary Jo White's decision not to include her in the prosecution, though surely she could have.

5. <u>Other unlawful uses of corporate funds for personal expenses.</u>

In her opening statement, Cathy Seibel, one of two Assistant U.S. Attorneys prosecuting the case, told the jury that the Pirros constructed a custom-built home, their present principal residence in Harrison, New York, in the late 80's. She went on to say, "Bills from the carpenters, plumbers, contractors, electricians, bills for utilities, landscapers, pool maintenance, exterminators, artwork, furniture, and accessories were all paid for by the businesses and illegally deducted."

Ms. Seibel then took the opportunity to single out one such expense, the installation of wrought iron, electrically controlled gates, which the Pirros had claimed were acquired as a security measure because of Mrs. Pirro's position as District Attorney. The gates cost $45,000. The Pirros had argued that the County of Westchester should have paid for them. However, as it turned out, the gates were not security gates, but decorative ones, and were actually planned before Jeanine was the District Attorney.

Given the cost of the gates, as well as the public attention they received, one might reasonably conclude that Jeanine Pirro surely should have been aware of how they were paid for, and from what source. The gates, however, were but one of several items purchased for her home for which evidence suggests she should have known the method of payment. There was also a certain $13,000 Chinese rug.

Using the services of an interior designer, Jeanine chose from among several offerings, that particular rug which she felt was best for her home. Given the time and the effort one may reasonably assume she invested in the search and selection, could she possibly not know the source of the funds which paid for it? Could she reasonably maintain her ignorance of the source of payment for such expensive personal items and expect to be believed?

6. "Under Penalty of Perjury"

Over the ten years between 1988 and 1997 Jeanine Pirro signed her name, as joint filer, to nine of ten fraudulent tax returns. Each and every one of those Form 1040 I.R.S. Tax Returns contained the following declaration above the signature line: "*Under penalty of perjury, I declare that I have examined this return, and accompanying schedules and statements, and to the best of my knowledge and belief, they are true, correct, and complete.*" While it is true that Jeanine was not placed on the stand, one may reasonably conclude that there was sufficient evidence that she committed perjury, particularly in light of Judge Barrington Parker's instruction to her husband's jury. Judge Parker instructed, "If an individual's name is signed to a return, it is evidence that the return was actually signed by him or her." Was this not a case of "What is sauce for the gander is sauce for the goose?"

Because the Government needs to prove beyond a reasonable doubt that a defendant tried for tax fraud, knew that he or she owed substantially more federal income taxes than was declared, and further acted willfully; one of the legal theories prosecutors employed against Al Pirro was "conscious avoidance." To be guilty of "conscious avoidance" requires only that a person is either aware that a materially important part of the tax return is wrong, and ignores it, or that there is a high probability that a person was aware that it was wrong. The Court also stated that guilt, "could be proven if a jury believed that a defendant acted with a conscious purpose to avoid learning the truth."

Clearly then, under the instructions given the jury which found her husband guilty, on all counts, of federal tax fraud, Jeanine Pirro would likely have been found guilty!

7. <u>The Hudson Valley Hospital Center (Peekskill Hospital) Affair</u>

Of all the criminal activity involving Albert J. Pirro, of which Jeanine Pirro was certainly aware, and was a direct beneficiary, clearly the scheme perpetrated against the community of Peekskill, in northern Westchester County, was the most egregious betrayal of the public treasury and the public trust. The charges were contained in Count 67 of the federal indictment. However, the facts were never brought out at trial because Judge Barrington Parker was concerned that to do so might have added two weeks to the proceedings. There is no dispute that the Government's charges were true, and well documented, involving criminal conduct mostly other than tax fraud.[9]

The facts surrounding the criminal transactions of Al Pirro and Robert Boyle, at the expense of the Peekskill community, are outrageous and depraved, and yet acceptable to Jeanine in her greed and lust for wealth. The Peeksill Hospital Affair, more than any other criminal scheme to enrich the Pirro household, is illustrative of why Jeanine Pirro is totally unfit to occupy the District Attorney's

Office. Let there be no mistake. Jeanine, by her certain knowledge of, and failure to prevent, prosecute, or seek a special prosecutor, was, in fact, a culpable conspirator and participant in the scheme which stole hundreds of thousands of dollars from the families of Peekskill.

What distinguishes Al Pirro's "rip-off" of the Hudson Valley Hospital Center, commonly referred to as Peekskill Hospital, from other white-collar criminal activities in which he has been involved, is the fact that in swindling the hospital Pirro and Boyle were really stealing from the hard-working people of Peekskill. They were stealing money which had been fund-raised and donated to the hospital in order that the sick, elderly, and injured might be cared for and restored to health, and they knew it. And, what's more shameful, so did Jeanine!

In February of 1991, Robert Boyle, a friend and business associate of Al Pirro, was the Chairman of the Board of Directors of Hudson Valley Hospital Center. Boyle brought to Al's attention the fact that there was a commercial building, which had previously housed a clock manufacturer, close to the hospital, available for purchase. Al wasted no time forming a corporation, Distinctive Properties of Croton Point, Inc., specifically to purchase and lease the property. However, the shareholders of the corporation were Paul Monsell, 10%, Albert Pirro, 45%, and Robert Boyle, 45%.

The purchase price of the building was $900,000, although the corporation secured a loan for $950,000 which was personally guaranteed by Pirro and Monsell. Robert Boyle made no cash or equity contribution to the corporation. Al Pirro would later try to claim, by doctoring up corporate papers, that he, in fact, owned 90% of the corporation and Monsell owned 10%, in a clumsy attempt to cover up the blatant conflict of interest at the core of the criminal scheme.

Without disclosure of Boyle's interest in the corporation to the other members of the hospital board, the hospital entered into an agreement to lease and to renovate the former clock company building, converting it into professional office space, and later purchasing it for 1.5 million dollars in July of 1993. The transactions clearly violated the law as they involved bribery, kick-back conspiracy, and breach of fiduciary responsibility. Over little more than two years, Al Pirro and Robert Boyle each profited by some $300,000 as a result of their unlawful conduct.

The significance of the Peekskill Hospital Affair is that it demonstrates the consequences of the circumstance which is created when a corrupt district attorney is the spouse of an individual who is actively engaged in unlawful activity. Jeanine had to be aware of the fact that her husband, and their good friend Robert Boyle were doing business with the Peekskill Hospital, and that Boyle was the Chairman of the Board of that institution. More importantly, she had to know that $300,000 of extra income had come into her household over a two year period, and that unlawful conduct had generated it.

Under the circumstances, Jeanine Pirro had a moral and a legal duty to prevent the victimization of the hospital and the Peekskill community. Having failed to prevent the scheme, she had a further legal duty, as district attorney, to seek the appointment of a special prosecutor, who would investigate and prosecute the crimes that she could not because of the obvious conflict of interest. Jeanine, of course, did nothing, preferring to sit on the information, until the five-year statute of limitations ran out. She was fully mindful of the fact that the transactions had been completed in 1993, just prior to her assuming office as district attorney, and that she could have discharged her legal obligation through 1998.

What makes Jeanine Pirro's failure to act in accordance with her legal duty as District Attorney of Westchester so egregious is the fact that she personally benefited from the fruits of the unlawful conduct of her husband and his co-conspirator. In effect, the moment Jeanine became District Attorney, Al Pirro and his associates were granted *de-facto immunity* from criminal prosecution.

It is worthy of note that had Jeanine elected to call for a "special prosecutor" at any time between 1995 and 1998, when the statute of limitations ran out, she would have had to approach Governor George Pataki. George Pataki was a member of the hospital board between 1991 and 1993 when the shameful "rip-off" was executed. George Pataki is the Governor who, prior to Al's conviction and Boyle's public disgrace, often boasted publicly that his "good friends Al Pirro and Robert Boyle" were his "biggest fund raisers." Apparently George Pataki took care of his good friends in kind.

No account of the trial, and its implications for Jeanine, would be complete without mention of her attempt to muzzle Professor Bennett Gershman of Pace University Law School. Prior to, and throughout the trial, local and regional press and broadcast media sought expert opinion regarding possible outcomes as well as the implication of evidence presented daily. Among the commentators most often questioned was Professor Gershman. He was well qualified, not only as a Professor of Law at Westchester's only law school, but more importantly as one who had been a special prosecutor with the late Frank Hogan, and as the author of *Prosecutorial Misconduct*, a widely read and acclaimed "Ten Commandments" for prosecutors.

When the trial was well under way, and Gershman, who had attended every day, had been quoted several times in the press, Jeanine, apparently no longer able to deal with it, went to the newly appointed dean of the law school, David Cohen. She threatened not to hire another Pace graduate if he did not "shut the professor's mouth." Just three years earlier, during her first re-election campaign, she declared, in *The New Yorker magazine,* "Freedom of Speech is alive and well in Westchester." Really, Jeanine?

||| Three |||

There's No Business Like Show Business

Jeanine Pirro's understanding of her position as District Attorney of Westchester has nothing whatever to do with public service, or dedication, or any sworn duty to her constituents. Jeanine perceives herself as a show business type celebrity, larger than life. It's an image she strains to maintain with excessive television, newspaper, and magazine exposure.

It would be an underestimate to suggest that Jeanine, in the course of any given year, makes three times the number of appearances in the media than all five New York City District Attorneys make combined. She is a "media hound" of the first magnitude, a fact which is not lost even on her dwindling supporters.

Jeanine's love affair with the camera got a big boost in her first term, as a nightly commentator on "Geraldo" and other shows during the O.J. Simpson trial. Attractive, and well spoken, if not always totally informed, she helped give some measure of "apparent authority" to the nightly O.J. national entertainment distraction. It was only natural that she should have linked-up with Geraldo, each, "So full of sound and fury, yet signifying nothing."

However, unlike Geraldo, her actual occupation, her sworn duty as a prosecutor, is not one normally intended to be so involved with, or compromised by, a narcissistic relationship with the camera. In fact, her constant misuse of the media and press, as a tool in the prosecution of defendants, frequently crosses the line from prosecutorial misconduct to unlawful behavior, as when she disregards judicial gag orders,[10] or leaks information about a grand jury subpoena. She attempts to achieve in the press what she is often unable to achieve in court.

In truth, the really great New York prosecutors over the past fifty years, Frank Hogan, Mario Merola, Robert Morganthau, and Jeanine's mentor and former employer, Carl Vergari, all avoided the limelight, performing their duties as prescribed by law. Jeanine, however enjoys a symbiotic relationship with the print and broadcast media. The importance of her constant hype and image projection is that it is central to the survival of the "Jeanine Machine."

It is difficult to estimate, fully, just how much of her eighteen million dollar annual budget is devoted to public relations, because just like her close friend, George Pataki, she disguises so much of her self-promotion in so-called public service releases. Given the salaries of those on staff specifically assigned to public relations - David Hebert, Ann Marie Corbalis, and others - plus mailings to the 365,000 Westchester households at $125,000 apiece, her publicly financed self-promotion probably exceeds a million dollars annually.

It is important to note that years ago when Jeanine asked the Westchester County Legislature for the funds to hire Hebert as her spokesman, they flatly refused the appropriation. Unaccustomed to not having her way, she hired him anyway, as an assistant district attorney, at a pay scale far above the position. She has proceeded to use him as her "mouthpiece" ever since, thumbing her nose at the legislators.

Sometimes Jeanine's symbiosis with television broadcasters can best be described as "Theatre of the Absurd," as, for example, her series of appearances on "Larry King Live" on CNN in January of 2002. The subject for discussion was Zacarias Moussaoui, the so-called "20th Terrorist," who was coming to trial in a federal court in Virginia. One of the issues discussed involved whether the presiding federal judge would, or should, allow television coverage from her courtroom.

The King format, as usual, included live phone calls with questions from viewers, and I would have posed two, had I been able to get through to him. "Mr. King, how do you justify the appearance of Jeanine Pirro on your program to discuss this matter when her only prosecutorial or judicial experience has been in state courts and her only recent appearance in federal court has been to observe the federal prosecution of her husband for income tax fraud?" My follow-up question would have been, "Don't you think it's somewhat inappropriate to ask Jeanine Pirro, who castigated the United States Attorney, Mary Jo White, who to date has been the most successful federal prosecutor of terrorists, given that the issue involves such a defendant?"

What was Larry King thinking about? He was thinking about three things, ratings, ratings, and ratings. Though the subject matter of his show often involves newsworthy information, and, in fairness, he has even presided over history-making confrontations, for the most part his highest priority is ratings. Not too surprisingly, Jeanine shares that same priority.

Jeanine appears largely out of touch with the impact her overexposure, especially on television, has had on many of her former supporters. Even if she is beginning to get the message, following the last election, it appears she can not help herself. She needs a constant "fix" to reassure her that she has not fallen off the public's radar screen. A case in point – Robert Durst.

In late October of 2001 Jeanine was engaged in the toughest campaign of her political life, against Tony Castro. With the only locally printed daily newspaper, *The Journal News,* comfortably in her pocket, she was refusing every proposed debate. She realized that she could not face Castro, a seasoned prosecutor with fourteen years experience before Bronx juries. There were simply too many unanswered questions about her culpable, hands-on involvement with her husband. Embarking upon a series of stalls and lies, which one columnist dubbed *The Debate Debate*, she caused a major rift within the ranks of the Westchester League of Women Voters by involving them in her divisive avoidance tactics. She desperately needed a distraction, something to take her away from Westchester. She found the perfect distraction in Robert Durst.

Durst, the heir to a real estate fortune in New York City, had been the subject of speculation and suspicion regarding the disappearance in 1982 of his young wife, a medical student, from their South Salem home in Northern Westchester. Several of her friends and family members had insisted over the years that Durst had killed her and disposed of the body. However, neither Carl Vergari, for more than a decade, nor Jeanine for eight years as D.A., was able to come up with sufficient evidence to bring charges.

The case would likely have remained dormant had it not been for the death of Susan Berman, in California, in December 2000, and a magazine article linking Berman to Durst and his missing wife. The article re-opened claims by friends and family that Cathy Durst had met with foul play at the hands of her very controlling husband.

With nothing, no new evidence, no charges to bring before a grand jury that could possibly result in an indictment, Jeanine Pirro jumped in. Why not? A lack of evidence never stood between Jeanine Pirro and a headline before. Why should it now, especially in an election year? Hey, you never know!

As it turned out, by October Robert Durst would be arrested in connection with a brutal murder and dismemberment of an elderly man in Galveston, Texas, and Jeanine would get her opportunity to do what she does best, -grab media attention. Two weeks before election, Jeanine, armed with nothing but her desire to make headlines while avoiding debate, flew to Galveston, taking a New York State Police Investigator and two assistant D.A.'s with her. Her action was totally unprecedented, and inappropriate, even had she brought charges before a grand jury and obtained an indictment. However, given that she lacked sufficient evidence even to bring charges, her trip to Texas was just one more hype and self- promotional opportunity at taxpayers' expense.

Not contented merely to grab the headlines while avoiding debating her opponent, Jeanine parlayed her Texas adventure into a major fundraising score, working in a little side excursion to Houston to pick up her largest individual campaign contribution, $24,500, from Hushang Ansary, an Arab oil magnate.

Of course, it is difficult to understand why an Arab oil magnate in Texas might have any particular interest in someone who is running for re-election to the D.A.'s Office in Westchester County, New York. But, then again, that's part of the enigma of the Jeanine Machine.

Perhaps the contribution was somehow connected to her declaration in angry tones, months earlier, on July 29, 2001, from the platform at the Arab-American Festival in Yonkers, "Remember, I am the only one who is exactly like you; not fifty percent, but one hundred percent like you." Of course, she was referring to her Lebanese ancestry. Interestingly, she made no such declaration, nor any attempt to reveal her ethnicity when lecturing a few weeks later on the subject of bias and hate crimes, at the Jewish Temple in Harrison,

New York. With Jeanine it's all about image versus reality.

So incessant and self-serving was Jeanine's pursuit of Durst for the headlines he might generate, that by December of 2001, his attorney Dick DeGuerin succeeded in persuading Texas State District Court Judge Susan Criss, to issue a "gag order," specifically naming Pirro. In his motion, DeGuerin accused her of "grandstanding and making egregious and outrageous statements," about his client, and "implying, with no supporting evidence, that he is a suspect in the disappearance of his wife, and the death of Susan Berman."

Unfortunately, Jeanine's insatiable hunger for headline coverage compels her to even defy judicial orders, and so she continued to show up in Pennsylvania and Texas. She attended extradition hearings and arraignments, at which she had no official business, specifically to get her face into camera range. Despite her conduct, prosecutors and police were courteous, but openly annoyed with her theatrics. Judge Criss was clearly upset by Jeanine's open defiance and disregard of her order, including an appearance on NBC's "Today Show," on January 25, 2002, to make defamatory and prejudicial statements about Durst.

In a feeble attempt to put a more favorable spin on Jeanine's antics, David Hebert, her mouthpiece, explained that her harassment of Durst was meant to "bring attention to the case for possible leaks." Hebert would go on to tell the *New York Times,* "It's crucial for law enforcement to have access to the media in order to highlight pending investigations and to encourage cooperation." Access to the media?

It is instructive to analyze what David Hebert, posing as something other than the public relations spinster he is, meant. As applied to Jeanine Pirro, "access to the media" is always for one, or both of two purposes. It is for self-promotion and/or public exposure and ridicule of her target. Her abuse of the press is facilitated by the fact that there is but one daily newspaper published in Westchester, *The Journal News*. As with any enterprise purporting to serve the public interest, the lack of competition within the marketplace invites, indeed, nurtures abuse.

As elaborate and persistent as Jeanine's ongoing year-round media presence may be, at election time it really goes into high gear. This is especially evident on radio, a medium she normally passes over, preferring, instead, the glitter and the theatrical opportunity only television can provide. Essentially it's a money thing, and the radio station management of several stations is clearly at fault for prostituting their newscasting operations for increased advertising revenues.

In the timeframe beginning in early September and running through Election Day, with increasing frequency and obviousness, several radio stations, all of which are airing her paid political spots, give strong coverage to even the most mundane and insignificant news releases from Pirro's office. The stations include, WCBS News Radio 880, 1010 WINS New York, ABC Radio, WHUD Peekskill, WFAS White Plains, and others. Of course, the practice is more obvious and offensive coming from the major players, CBS, WINS, and ABC, given that the local stations are normally more concerned with Westchester news items, and are more likely to give her coverage year-round.

It's a simple matter of "bottom-line," low integrity broadcasting. Jeanine spends tens of thousands of dollars at each station, literally saturating the airwaves with her campaign propaganda, and the stations, in turn, give coverage to her every press release as though it had come from the White House. By Mid-October listeners are virtually inundated with Jeanine Pirro round the clock.

The air-time does not come cheaply. It costs as much as $800 to $1,000 per minute in prime time slots. Is it probably overkill? Sure. But, to a media-hound such as Jeanine, overkill is the last consideration. It's show business, after all, and, as the expression goes, "The show must go on!"

||| Four |||

Vixen In The Hen House

Jeanine Pirro truly believes that nobody seriously has the right to run against her. She suffers from the malady known as "being a legend in your own mind." Having nearly been turned out of office by a virtual unknown, Tony Castro, caused more damage than her fragile ego could tolerate without exacting revenge. She believed that the race for District Attorney of Westchester, in 2001, was going to bring out a Democratic candidate who would not seriously challenge her throne.

Jeanine believed that she would be easily re-elected D.A. as a Republican, cleansing her of the tax fraud scandal, and Andy Spano would be easily re-elected County Executive, as a Democrat. The only problem was that Tony Castro wasn't in on the deal. Tony was serious, so serious that five months prior to election he resigned his position as Deputy Chief of Homicides and the Grand Jury in the Bronx District Attorney's Office. He had worked there for fourteen years.

Nevertheless, there was a deal, (one which will be fully detailed), and Jeanine was prepared to bring pressure, if necessary, to enforce it. The person she would bring her grievance to was her long-time friend and mutual beneficiary of the deal, Andy Spano. The traditional rules of adversarial campaign conduct were off the table, and party loyalty and integrity were, as had often been the case in Westchester politics, mere naïve concepts.

It was just such an 'unholy alliance,' her deal with Andy Spano, which would bring about one of Jeanine Pirro's more vindictive, abusive, and unlawful exercises of prosecutorial misconduct to date, the Jay Hashmall Affair. From Jeanine's point of view "a deal was a deal," and she expected Andy to exercise the same absolute control over his deputies that she exercised over hers. Their powers in the Westchester political arena could be likened to the King and the Queen in a game of chess. As anyone who has ever played knows, the ultimate power resides with the Queen.

For Jeanine Pirro a "fixed election" was no great leap. After all, she is the wife of Al Pirro, a fixer of great note in the Westchester business community, a man with his hand in your pocket, a man who had "brought home the bacon," with deals like the Peekskill Hospital Swindle, with her blessings and protection. Given the fact that she was running for re-election as the chief law enforcement officer of the County, and the man she had been married to for more than twenty years was away in federal prison for crimes they had committed as co-conspirators, a fixed election scheme was really no problem for Jeanine at all!

As the campaign entered the final three months, and Tony Castro was beginning to look like he might be a problem for her, Jeanine became intolerant of what she perceived as breaches within her ranks. Of course, her concept of who was within her ranks included persons no rational individual would have counted on, persons she had no right to expect to control. Two such individuals were Jay Hashmall, Deputy County Executive, under Andy Spano, and Robi Schlaff, a high ranking assistant who worked closely with Hashmall as a liaison to the Public Works Department, each very active in the Westchester Democratic Party. While she certainly could not expect to control their votes, Jeanine would absolutely not tolerate their open support of and assistance to her opponent, Tony Castro. She had cut a deal with their boss, Andy Spano, and they would obey, or else!

By mid-August it was no secret that Jay was actively supporting and advising Tony Castro, even going so far as to procure and provide statistical information from the County's Human Resources files regarding the make-up of Jeanine's staff.[11] That assistance drew an angry call to Andy Spano, warning of severe consequences. But neither Jay, nor Robi, had any intention of 'kissing Jeanine's ring.'

Quite to the contrary, they planned and carried out an excellent fund-raiser at Robi's home some weeks later. Jeanine was livid, and God only knows what wrath she breathed at Andy. No matter, Jay and Robi were in her 'cross-hairs' and revenge was a certainty.

I had just left my employment with a White Plains law office, to join the Castro Campaign full-time as Campaign Director, in early August. The first word of Jeanine's protest to Andy Spano seemed absurd, even for her. I was not, yet, aware of the extent of the deal and the bond between them. But, knowing her M.O., it seemed to me that Jeanine had to be armed with something stronger on Andy than "a deal is a deal."

In the dozen or so weeks to election, Tony and I, and a handful of campaign workers closest to the action, were surely aware that if she survived, Jeanine would have her revenge. We simply couldn't imagine the issue. We were confident that Jay had done nothing to break the law. However, that never stopped Jeanine before.

A few days before the election *The Journal News* published a front page article raising questions about four no-bid contracts which had been awarded by the County between December of 1998 and August of 2001, to one contractor, Ralph Arred. Mr. Arred was a former chairman of the Yonkers Democratic City Committee, and a former legal client of Jay Hashmall.

The contracts had been awarded under County Rules, which permit no-bid contracts to be let out by the County Board of Acquisition and Contract, a three- member board consisting of the county executive and two legislators. Under the rules, when an emergency condition is declared, and the bidding process might delay prompt attention and needed repairs, contracts may be awarded without competitive bidding. Each of the projects which had been awarded to Arred involved unsafe conditions, which, if left unattended to, might have subjected the County to legal liability and costly litigation.

Ordinarily, under the rules, the county executive is required to sign-off, together with the two members of the legislature, unless he is unavailable. In his absence, his deputy, Jay Hashmall, would be required to act in his stead. Interestingly, Andy Spano, although not out of town, was "unavailable" to vote on each of the contracts awarded to Ralph Arred.

When the first article appeared in *The Journal News* there was no question "the second shoe had fallen." Jeanine Pirro had threatened reprisal, and this was reprisal! This was a classic Jeanine "Prosecution in the Press." We knew it would only be a matter of time before word would come out that a grand jury was convening to investigate some alleged wrongdoing by Jay Hashmall, and possibly others.

The only surprise came in the swiftness, just a few days following the first article, with which the next article appeared. It proclaimed that grand jury subpoenas had been issued to Jay and others. Jeanine had delivered on her threat.

First she implied the convening of a grand jury without one shred of evidence of any unlawful activity and issued subpoenas. Then, she leaked those activities to the public via *The Journal News,* her propaganda arm. She had gotten even with Hashmall and others who had *had the nerve to support her Democratic opponent,*

Tony Castro. She could care less that her activities were unlawful prosecutorial misconduct. Vengeance was hers, and Jay Hashmall's reputation would be forever tainted.

Once again Jeanine Pirro had violated the civil rights of an individual who had dared to stand up to her tyranny. She saw fit to abuse the powers of her office, this time to compromise the confidentiality of grand jury subpoenas guaranteed by state and federal constitutional statute.

Within days of the leaks, two facts were clear. Jeanine had extracted her revenge, and Jay Hashmall, and possibly others, would likely lose their jobs. As if to help insure the latter outcome, *The Journal News* continued to rehash the story, day after day. Although it was apparent that no crime had been committed, no breach of regulations had occurred, and the District Attorney had brought no charges, a steady stream of articles appeared.

Nevertheless, Andy Spano, who had just been re-elected County Executive of Westchester, with 72% of the vote, asked for, and received Jay Hashmall's resignation. Several days later, about the first week of December, Robi Schlaff, who had not been connected to the no-bid awards, was also asked to resign. Each had been punished, under color of law, for having exercised their constitutionally guaranteed Rights of Free Speech and Freedom of Association.

The Jeanine Machine had narrowly survived the election, and in her 'heart of hearts' Jeanine knew she had no mandate. She knew, as those of us close to the action realized on Election Night, that she had won by extortion. Still, she defied all reality, returning to her unlawful and vindictive self in her assaults on Hashmall and Schlaff.

Her dominion over the press was not limited to *The Journal*

News. The persistence of the Hashmall story in that paper stimulated interest by a feature writer for the *New York Law Journal.* She had covered the debate controversy shortly before the election.

The writer, Lori Tripoli, contacted Tony Castro requesting a "Letter to the Editor" which would explain events concerning the Jay Hashmall Affair from Tony's perspective. Tony agreed to submit it, and a brief note appeared in the *Law Journal* the following day, promising Tony's response. Tony was pleased for the opportunity to inform the readership of the *Law Journal* of the true nature of Jeanine's activities against Hashmall and others. However, within 24 hours Tony was called and was told that once Jeanine got wind of the fact that there would be a forthcoming article, she contacted someone very high in management, and quashed the piece.

Immediately, upon learning of the *New York Law Journal's* knuckling-under to Jeanine's pressure I attempted to contact Dorothy Samuels of the *New York Times,* the editor who had interviewed Tony prior to his receiving their endorsement. She couldn't get off the phone fast enough. I was left with a sick feeling.

My senses told me Jeanine had reached them too. My fears were fueled by the fact that, although Tony had received the prized *Times* endorsement following a 90 minute interview, which I had attended, that endorsement was eight days in coming. Further, it appeared just three days before election, leaving us little time or opportunity to capitalize on it. As importantly, on the day that it did appear, their Metro-Section reporter in Westchester, Randal C. Archibold, ran a feature story on Jeanine, including a photo with a "horse laughing face" predicting that she would easily win.

In the moments following Ms. Samuel's 'virtual hang-up', and on the heels of the *Law Journal's* capitulation, the notion that a book needed to be written was born. It was only a few weeks following her re-election by the narrowest of margins yet and still it was "business as usual." I had a decision to make. Either I would be part of the solution or part of the problem.

Interestingly, several weeks after the initial leaks to them, *The Journal News* published a full two-page article detailing Jay Hashmall's career in Westchester and Yonkers City government. The paper took great care to make it appear that the "no-bid issue" had somehow come to their attention from thin air, and that as a result of their 'spontaneous discovery' the D.A.'s Office immediately convened a grand jury and issued subpoenas to Hashmall and others. The simple fact was that no evidence ever was, or ever would be, presented to a grand jury because no crime was committed. Therefore, a grand jury would be compelled to return "no true bill," putting an end to Jeanine Pirro's harassment of Jay Hashmall.

Those observers familiar with the process know that conducting an investigation, preparing a presentation and convening a grand jury to receive charges, could not have occurred in the few days between the first two articles, as Jeanine and *The Journal News* would have everyone believe. Quite simply, Jeanine abused her prosecutorial powers by involving *The Journal News*, which was only too happy to be the conduit for her malicious message.

Another interesting aspect of the Hashmall story, not covered by *The Journal News*, or any other source, was the fact that Andy Spano had also been served with a subpoena by Jeanine, in connection with her "no-bid grand jury investigation." However, Spano managed to get his subpoena quashed by a County Judge, with no meaningful resistance by her, a fact which also went unreported.

Following his forced resignation, Jay Hashmall, a Democrat, whose service in several capacities to the Yonkers City Government spanned more than twenty years, was asked by the Republican mayor, John Spencer, to serve as Commissioner of Human Resources. The position paid $122,000 annually, and, under City Charter Rules was subject to ratification by the City Council if the Council members chose to exercise that option. Otherwise, if no action were to be taken by that body, the appointment would become permanent after forty-five days.

As the forty-five day period was about over, it appeared that the City Council would permit the appointment to stand. Of the seven council members, three had indicated that if brought to a vote they would approve. Two had said they were not in favor, and two claimed to be undecided. Jeanine could not find it within herself to stop harassing Jay Hashmall for having supported her Democratic opponent. She would find some way to influence the Yonkers City Council.

Within a few days of the deadline, Jeanine fired off a subpoena to Gordon Burrows, a Republican Council Member. The subpoena demanded production of the minutes of a meeting with the Council on January 22, 2002, at which Hashmall had been questioned, amongst other issues, about the circumstances surrounding the no-bid contracts. The meeting and the minutes of the meeting were available to the public. Jeanine was, once again, engaging in drama and overkill, using the power of her office in an abusive manner. She used a subpoena to suggest to the Council and to the public that there was an actual grand jury investigation in progress, and that information seeking an indictment had been put before a grand jury.

Nothing could have been further from the truth. If Jay Hashmall had committed an indictable act, Jeanine Pirro would surely have sought that indictment. She knew that what Jay had done was fully in accordance with County Rules, and that the necessity for him to have acted at all, was brought about by the intentional absence of her co-conspirator, County Executive Andy Spano. If she thought she had even a prayer of indicting Jay Hashmall she would have stubbornly resisted Andy Spano's attempt to quash his subpoena in December.

Jeanine, however, knew she could count on Vincenza "Vinny" Restiano, City Council President, to do her dirty work for her. Restiano had claimed to be undecided, but in reality, was against Hashmall and Mayor Spencer.[12] The only truly undecided Council Member was Sandy Anabi, a newly elected member whose skin was still too tender to withstand the "heat in the kitchen." Well-intentioned as she might have been, Councilwoman Anabi was pressured into voting against Jay Hashmall, an innocent public servant with a twenty- year history of service to her city, because of accusation and innuendo, none of which had ever been presented to a grand jury. Whatever became of "Innocent until proven guilty?"

On March 12, 2002, Mayor Spencer snatched victory from Jeanine's vindictive claws, appointing Jay Hashmall as his Second Deputy Mayor, at $128,000 per year. Appointments of deputy mayors in Yonkers, as in most major cities, are not subject to City Council Ratification. However, although he has secured meaningful well-paid employment with the City of Yonkers for the next two years, Jay Hashmall's good name, with his career in public life, and as an attorney, have been seriously maligned.

The intentional and malicious damage to Hashmall's reputation and standing within the community, as well as the pain and humiliation he, his wife, and two children continue to suffer at the hands of Jeanine Pirro, cry out for legal remedy. Jeanine's behavior, under color of law, would be a clear cause of action under U.S. 42 Sec.1983. Under Sec.1983, a citizen may bring an action against a state official who violates his constitutional rights "under color of law." By using the power of her office to harass and punish Mr. Hashmall, Jeanine Pirro has engaged in prosecutorial misconduct not covered by the 'absolute immunity,' normally conferred upon prosecutors in their legitimate judicial activities.

At best, she might enjoy only 'qualified immunity' for her legitimate administrative and investigative activities, a proposition long settled in the decisions of the United States Supreme Court. However, her leaks of information to *The Journal News* are clearly unlawful conduct enjoying no prosecutorial immunity whatsoever!

If it were demonstrated that Jeanine Pirro used the power of her office to deny Jay Hashmall the Rights of Freedom of Speech, Freedom of Association and Assembly, as well as the Rights to Employment and Property, she and Westchester County would be in serious legal trouble, indeed. And Andy Spano would surely be in the thick of it for his willing role in all of it.

||| Five |||

The Cabal

Attorney Orlando: "Isn't it a fact that sometimes the Republicans and the Democrats (in Westchester) work together to achieve an election result?"

Election Commissioner Sunderland: "Yes."

Attorney Orlando: "Isn't it a fact that Republicans and Democrats are not always adversaries?"

Election Commissioner Sunderland: "Yes."

This exchange, on cross-examination, of Westchester County Republican Election Commissioner Carolee Sunderland by defense attorney Geoffrey Orlando at the election fraud trial of Dennis Wedra, in Westchester County Court on February 1, 2002, certainly says it all.

If there were any voters in Westchester still laboring under the impression that fixed elections didn't happen there, Commission Sunderland set the record straight. She delivered her response as matter-of-factly as if she were offering the time of day. There was no reluctance, no hesitation to acknowledge that the system, the electoral process over which she had been a guardian for more than twelve years, had, on numerous occasions, been dysfunctional.

She had sworn to "tell the truth, the whole truth, and nothing but the truth." Therefore, it must be accepted that as between Democrats and Republicans seeking public office in Westchester, all is not necessarily always what it might appear. In fact, it would be most accurate to state that for about the last eight years the election process in Westchester, indeed, the political machinery as it pertains to the highest offices, has been under the influence, if not the control, of a cabal.

The dictionary defines a cabal as follows: "***Cabal - a secret group of plotters or political conspirators.***" In Westchester County politics there is a cabal, which can be best described as a wheel, the hub of which is District Attorney Jeanine Pirro. Clearly, every other member, political office holders, newspaper publishers, party chairpersons, lobbyists, and judges, are all subordinate to one more powerful than they, Jeanine Pirro. She derives her supreme power from her unique role within the jurisdiction. She is the only one with the power to prosecute. She alone has the vested authority and machinery to lawfully or unlawfully, destroy any or all of the other members of The Cabal, or anyone else she may want to.

So awesome is the power of a prosecutor that citizens need to be more thoughtful and cautious about whom they are willing to entrust with it. Unfortunately, many otherwise intelligent voters will often assume that a district attorney is someone only criminals need be concerned about. Nothing could be further from the truth. The vested authority to investigate, indict, and prosecute was never intended to fall into the hands of a self-promoting, unindicted co-conspirator the likes of Jeanine Pirro!

She is at the center of the Cabal calling the shots, because she, and she alone, can use the information known amongst all of the members against them, while remaining free from retaliatory attack herself. She can, by mere threat of indictment, cause even the most highly held and influential political member to bend to her will, precisely as she made Andy Spano do in the Jay Hashmall Affair.

Only the most naïve observer would believe that Jay Hashmall and Robi Schlaff lost their high-paying positions in Andy Spano's administration for any reason other than the fact that Andy was compelled to fulfill Jeanine's desire to take vengeance against them. In effect, it was their heads . . . or his.

If not for her power to prosecute, why else would a man, who had just received 72% of the vote for County Executive, kneel before the will of a district attorney who won by only 6%, and who needed to extort nearly 8,000 votes to do it? Despite all that Jeanine and Andy must have on each other, it is only she who can indict, and prosecute. In reality, except for her power to intimidate him, why should Andy Spano, a very popular county executive, who had presided over three property tax reductions in a row, have needed to agree to enter into a fixed election scheme? Why, indeed, when the sole purpose of that scheme was to re-elect a district attorney whose husband was in federal prison doing time for income tax fraud which most people acknowledge she had had a hand in?

The sad truth is that Jeanine must have such stuff on Andy Spano that he was not only willing to sell-out his own running mate, Tony Castro, in advance, but to genuflect before her, and fire two of his most talented and capable deputies, because they refused to. Of course, as Andy would discover, the fact has not been lost on many Democrats that he not only sold-out Tony, but also sold them out as well.

The Cabal is not about party. Quite the opposite, it crosses party affiliation, and thus deliberately conspires to deceive and defraud the voting public, the 365,000 households within Westchester. The cabal is about so much more than the usual "You scratch my back, and I'll scratch yours." It is about defrauding and raping the people, and the institutions, of Westchester, as in the Peekskill Hospital Swindle. It is about control — control of the press, the media, the machinery of government, and those institutions that are supposed to protect every-day citizens from fraud, larceny, and disenfranchisement.

The Cabal is the ultimate corruption. It is the most perverted exploitation of our free system of government, right at home in Westchester. It is the very heart of the Jeanine Machine.

One of the more prominent members of The Cabal is State Senator Nick Spano, one of sixteen children, and the son of County Clerk Len Spano, another Cabal member. We are told that this Spano clan is no relation to Andy. However, State Senator or not, Nick Spano is obedient to and cooperative with Jeanine. A popular politician, particularly in Italian-American circles, Nick is always ready to lend Jeanine a hand. So it was with great interest that I attended the trial of Dennis Wedra for more than a week, knowing that Nick Spano and his re-election effort of 2000 might figure prominently in the testimony of the case.

Before the trial began, I wondered why Jeanine would want to perform such delicate prosecutorial surgery. On the one hand she was going after Wedra, and the Democratic Club of Yonkers, and on the other, possibly implicating and injuring her 'buddy' Nick. My puzzlement was soon resolved. Jeanine had a more than usual desire, a personal desire, to hurt Dennis Wedra, as was revealed in the first few days of testimony.

Apparently, a tape which was produced by a corrupt, former candidate for City Court Judge of Yonkers, Philip Werbel, who wore a wire for Jeanine, contained a remark by Wedra, actually intended to describe one of her female investigators. She had gone unannounced, together with three of her male counterparts, to

Wedra's apartment, on a 'fishing expedition' the day after Wedra had buried his girlfriend of many years, back in April of 2000. In mourning for his companion, who had suffered with cancer, Wedra was angered by the intentional timing of the 'raid' and referred to the woman as a "fucking cunt." In listening to the tape, Jeanine took it as a reference to herself.

Thin-skinned as she is, Jeanine was determined to get even. She was equally determined to damage the Democratic Club of Yonkers, and to instill fear and respect in politicos throughout the county. Stacked up against these objectives, any concern she might have had about implicating 'Senator Nick' was of little importance to Jeanine.

Wedra, a man about 60, who had been a community activist and public servant for many years, as well as a political consultant, had been indicted on 166 counts of election fraud. The case involved some forty "absentee voters" in the southwest precincts of the City of Yonkers, mostly Latinos. It was alleged by Werbel and Anthony Mangone, Senator Spano's chief of staff, that Wedra, who had been hired by Werbel and by the Senator, had directed Werbel and Mangone to falsify and alter ballots.

In fact, Nick Spano was engaged in a tough election campaign against Tom Abinanti, a Democratic county legislator, who was seeking Spano's senate seat. Nick needed all of the independent political lines he could get. He was trying to 'harvest' Green Party and Independence Party votes.

New York State is one of the few states which permits candidates for public office to run on more than one line, a fact which causes a disproportionately great amount of time, money, and effort to be expended securing such minor party endorsements. However small the number of votes garnered on minor party lines may be, it has often represented the margin of victory in close contests, a fact that causes many candidates to "do whatever it takes." Such was the scenario in the contest for district attorney between Jeanine Pirro and Tony Castro, as will be discussed further on.

Jeanine Pirro's case against Dennis Wedra was remarkably weak, even for her office. She is notorious for overcharging defendants, coming up short on evidence, and using "smoke and mirrors" to convince juries. She also tries to persuade juries with her presence in the courtroom, often several times, at key points in a trial.

In the Wedra case, she had taken a plea from Werbel the "judge candidate," to "Tampering With An Election," a misdemeanor, and persuaded him to wear a wire. Really unsatisfied with that taping and unable to produce one piece of tangible evidence linking Dennis Wedra to tampering or altering of ballots, she took nearly eighteen months to bring the case to trial. However, Jeanine's reluctance to move the case along, even in the face of newspaper editorials six months earlier, calling for prompt disposition, was not so much about the weakness or the poor preparation of her case as it was about her own political agenda. As will be explained, Jeanine Pirro did not want the election fraud matter disposed of before she would run for re-election in 2001.

At trial, her deputies, Mr. Sassloff and Mr. Landes, of her "Public Integrity Unit," (almost an oxymoronic title to be associated with Jeanine) were trying to sell the jury a theory of *guilt by association* mixed with a helping of *guilt for foul language.* Neither theory impressed the jury which was comprised of five Latinos (two men and three women), two Blacks (a man and a woman, each about 70) and the remainder, mostly women between 30 and 70, all basically working class individuals.

The logic of the Prosecution's argument went, essentially, "Hey, look, we have these two guys, Werbel and Mangone. One is a candidate just dying to be a judge somewhere, anywhere, and the other is the 'Wonderchild' advisor to 'big, but not too bright,' Senator Spano. They are willing to plead guilty for a slap on their wrists, and blame everything they did on Mr. Wedra. Now, if they are willing to admit that they are guilty of election 'hanky-panky' Wedra must also be guilty, although neither can testify under oath that they ever saw him do anything illegal."

If that argument was not convincing enough, there was also, "Listen folks, we don't like having to play that secretly recorded tape with all those dirty words for you. And, we don't like saying those words at every opportunity to you. And, we don't enjoy projecting them on the wall for you to read. But, we need to show you how guilty Mr. Wedra must be."

Throughout the trial the jury did not appear too intrigued by the prosecution's case. A few were actually falling asleep at points. To Jeanine's dismay, they were also not impressed when she walked into the courtroom, for a second time, about twenty minutes into the defense counsel's summation. She was wearing four-inch stiletto heels, a miniskirt, and dark stockings with white embroidery. When she arrived, there were already nine Assistant D.A.'s and investigators crammed into the small courtroom, all duly noted by defense counsel.

Would any other district attorney be doing business this way? Not if they were conducting a serious prosecution of election fraud, in a dignified and reasonable fashion. However, Jeanine Pirro is neither dignified, nor reasonable. Once again, <u>it is all about image versus reality.</u> She is so accustomed to having things her way, she does not realize that people are becoming wise to her, and turned-off by her antics.

Jeanine would have had the jury believe that she was a sincere spokesperson for the rights of voters, an advocate for honesty in the election process. In reality she is the ringleader of a most corrupt cabal, fixing and manipulating elections, at the highest levels of Westchester Government, and using the power of her office to keep it so. A conviction of Dennis Wedra would have kept all of her "subjects" in fear. She would continue to reign supreme, her power and authority once again affirmed.

Jeanine had one problem, though.. This jury wasn't buying her case. In fact, they weren't buying her! As it turned out, after acquitting Wedra on all counts, the jurors waited outside the courthouse to congratulate him. As they told reporters, they "did not accept the District Attorney's version, nor the way it was presented."

The jury didn't like the selective prosecution of one man for the crimes committed by two others, whom Jeanine had allowed to get off easy, when, in fact, they had been motivated by self-interest and greed[13]. They saw through the lack of evidence and the maliciousness of the prosecution. They said, *Tell it to the Marines, Jeanine!*

Upon the conclusion of the trial, I was reminded of a statement Dhyalma Vazquez, of the Independence Party, (who had made the original complaint of election fraud in April of 2000), had given to reporters in February of 2001. She had criticized Jeanine Pirro publicly for her refusal to bring the election fraud case to trial before the elections of 2001. Vazquez said, "to make waves now, and prosecute Democrats and Republicans, and her fellow landsmen in the Independence Party, would be a major blow for her chances to get re-elected." How very close to the target she came.

Given what her office brought to court in the way of evidence, the hollowness and deceitfulness of Jeanine's response to Ms. Vazquez' statement through her mouthpiece, David Hebert, is very transparent. He told *The Journal News,* "We are going to follow every investigative lead, and take it to its conclusion, regardless of where it takes us, or how long it takes us." He went on, "I'm confident that at the conclusion of our investigation, the public will fully understand the scope and thoroughness of our investigation." They surely did.

Within a few days following the jury's rebuke of Jeanine Pirro, Ron Patafio, Editorial Page Editor of *The Journal News*, with the clear support of his employer, Gary F. Sherlock, attempted to put a favorable spin on events. Of course, those familiar with the role of *The Journal News* throughout the campaign of 2001 for district attorney, know that Patafio and Sherlock have been willing and eager members of The Cabal for some time. Gary Sherlock is more than just a golf-buddy to Al Pirro.

In an editorial entitled "Manipulated Election," which appeared on Tuesday, February 12, 2002, Patafio's subtitle declared, "Wedra Trial Gave Public An Inside Look At Politics At Its Very Worst." No truer words were ever spoken. However, not as applied to the prosecuted, but rather to the prosecutor.

The truly manipulated election was not the election of 2000. It was the election of 2001, for district attorney. The manipulator was Jeanine Pirro herself, who extorted the endorsement of the Independence Party, by threatening to indict and include a leader of the party, Dr. Giullio Cavallo, in the election fraud case she would ultimately bring against Dennis Wedra. At trial it was revealed that some of the fraudulently filed Green Party absentee ballots, which had been confiscated, also contained votes cast for candidates on the Independence Party line.

In 1997, Jeanine Pirro, in her first bid for re-election, received the endorsement of the Independence Party, which brought some 5,800 votes. Within weeks of that election Jeanine and Al knew they had mounting legal problems, which the public was not yet aware of. Jeanine won her race against Joann Naughten by a margin of 2 to 1. Naughten had spent exactly $3,000 and received what everyone conceded was the "core Democratic vote."

On the evening of May 24, 2001, Tony Castro received the nomination of the Westchester County Democratic Committee for District Attorney of Westchester, to run against incumbent Jeanine Pirro. That same day, at 2PM, Castro had met with Dr. Cavallo, Dhyalma Vazquez, and Mario Castaldo, leaders of the Independence Party. After interviewing him, and reviewing his experience, and his position on major issues, as well as his plans for the office, they told him they would endorse him for District Attorney. Each of them offered their business and their cell-phone numbers to Castro.

Then, as they were about to part company, Cavallo said, "We want to endorse you, but we have to put this before our committee. She scares and intimidates us." Tony Castro never heard another word from the Independence Party. Two weeks later, *The Journal News* proclaimed, "Independence Party Endorses Pirro."

There is always a method to Jeanine's madness. There was a reason why she postponed the election fraud trial for 18 months, and it had nothing to do with completing her investigation. She came to court, even after all that time, empty. The reason for her delay became obvious at trial. It had to do with the fact that some of the fraudulent absentee-ballots that had been punched with votes for Senator Nick Spano and Philip Werbel on the Green

Party line, had also been punched for candidates on the Independence Party line.

Jeanine Pirro knew very well that those punches were not the work of Cavallo, or any of his party members. But, that didn't stop her from intimidating those people with threats to indict them and drag them into the case. She knew that she needed every vote she could get, by whatever means necessary.

The sad truth is that by allowing her to extort their endorsement, the Independence Party handed Jeanine Pirro the election. Without their endorsement, she would have lost by nearly 4,000 votes. More than 7,800 votes were cast on the Independence Party line.

Two days after the election, Tony Castro and I paid a visit to the Democratic Commissioner of Elections, Reggie Lafayette. He greeted us with news that he had received a call earlier in the day from Dr. Cavallo who told him how very much he regretted having given Jeanine Pirro the Independence Party's endorsement, because he realized that it cost Tony Castro the election. Lafayette went on to say that Cavallo told him, "She scared and intimidated us." Tony had heard those very words before, "from the horse's mouth."

It is important to distinguish The Cabal from *the Jeanine Machine*. The *Jeanine Machine* includes The Cabal, but is a broader less intensely focused confederation of individuals, both in and outside of Westchester, and Westchester politics. Many members of the Machine are well-meaning (if misled) supporters of Jeanine, who have bought into her myth. Good examples might be Larry King or Ed Koch.

The Cabal by contrast, consists of a small group within the Machine who clearly know who Jeanine really is and who, for their own gain, have chosen to aid and abet her mission. These individuals are the most dangerous to the community. They know the lie and the subversion of the justice system and the political process to which Jeanine is committed, and they willingly join her as co-conspirators against us all.

It is instructive to recognize some of the other members of The Cabal. Each of Jeanine's paid mouthpieces, David Hebert, hired against the wishes of the county legislature specifically to be her spokesperson, Ann Marie Corbalis, in charge of public relations, and Sarah Gaffney Mahoney, her campaign strategist, are also close to the myth, and the lie that is churned out every day. Given their task, they have a great subject to work with. She is a great actress. But she is more. She is the perfect socio-path, lacking all conscience.

It would be unfair to Andy Spano, already adequately recognized as a major member of The Cabal, to neglect to include Larry Schwartz, his "Svengali." Surely, Andy would not be in the position he is in today if not for Larry, as Larry is quick to tell everyone. People close to them did not need a *New York Times* profile of Larry to know that he has been the "brains" behind the operation. Naturally, Andy's "Deal with the Devil," had Larry's fingerprints all over it.

Then there is Mike Edelman, former law partner of Al Pirro, Republican Political Analyst for Cable Television News Channel 12, and spinmaster for the Jeanine Machine. It was Mike Edelman in an article in *The Journal News*, of course, who proclaimed that New York State's legislators, "could hardly wait for Al Pirro to emerge" 18 months early from federal prison so he could lobby them. The man simply has no morals, no conscience, and no credibility where Albert and Jeanine Pirro are concerned.

Robert Boyle, disgraced former Chairman of The Port of New York Authority, and Al's 'partner in crime' in the Peekskill Hospital Swindle, surely qualifies as a cabal member, if somewhat less active following his exposure.

Moving a little further upstate, there's Dennis Vacco, New York State Attorney General from 1994 to 1998. His protective blanket kept Al and Boyle from prosecution, much as Jeanine did, by allowing the statute of limitations to run out in the hospital case, and by finding "insufficient evidence to prosecute" Al in an earlier bribery case in Yonkers in which Al was accused of paying-off a Planning Commission member to get a theater complex approved.

Then there is Governor George Pataki — and that's no stretch. Pataki has boasted of his close relationship with the Pirros for years. On numerous occasions (he probably wishes he could take back), Pataki praised Al Pirro and Robert Boyle as his biggest fundraisers. And, as previously noted, he was on the board of directors of the hospital when they pulled off their swindle.

It is not so shocking that George Pataki should be associated with the likes of the Pirros. After all wasn't Pataki's mentor, Al D'Amato, one of the biggest mobsters to ever sit in the United States Senate? They didn't call him "Teflon Al" for nothing. He even skated when his brother Armand went to prison for trying to influence him.

Supposedly, George Pataki had a deal with Jeanine, going into the last election. The word is, although not verified, that Jeanine needed to muster at least 58% of the vote in order to be considered for Lieutenant Governor in 2002. Those closest to Jeanine have acknowledged that she was seeking a convincing victory in order to "cleanse herself" of the tax fraud scandal, and keep her hopes of higher office alive. Having won with only 52%, it would appear that she failed with both objectives.

Still, in late March of 2002, the all-too-familiar Jeanine Pirro trial- balloons were already taking flight. Rumors of her possible candidacy for the second spot on Pataki's ticket were becoming more frequent. Interestingly, in early April, Pataki, who had not officially announced his own candidacy, felt the need to declare that he intended to rename his current lieutenant if he decided to go for a third term.

Irrespective of Pataki's intentions regarding Jeanine, it is interesting that his campaign strategist, Kieran Mahoney, just happens to have run Jeanine's 1997 campaign, and is the husband of Sarah Gaffney Mahoney. The Mahoneys are well matched to the candidates they advise — Jeanine Pirro, George Pataki, Al D'Amato, and Dennis Vacco. Their "Brezhnev Doctrine: What's mine is mine, and what's yours we'll talk about," is so absolutely suited to such greedy, culpable counterfeits. "Show me your friends and I'll tell you who you are."

An interesting postscript to the Wedra trial appeared in *The Journal News* on April 4, 2002. In a front page article entitled "Vote Fraud Aide Hired By Pirro Attorneys," reporter Bruce Golding reported, "A political aide, who tampered with absentee votes, but was not indicted, is now working for a law firm that represented the husband of District Attorney Jeanine Pirro, in his tax fraud case."

The report goes on to state, "Anthony Mangone, part-time counsel to State Senator Nick Spano, has been employed by Servino, Santangelo, and Randazzo. The office is in a converted three-family house, owned by the District Attorney's husband Al Pirro. He has been running a lobbying business out of the building since his November release from a federal prison camp."

Questioned by reporter Golding, Jeanine Pirro responded, "I am unaware that Mr. Mangone is working in my husband's building. Mr. Mangone's job there is unrelated to his deal with my office." Sure Jeanine, and you also didn't know what was in all of those fraudulent tax returns you signed.

||| Six |||

Hear No Evil, See No Evil

Few areas of criminal prosecution illustrate the complete inappropriateness and fraudulence of Jeanine Pirro's occupation of the Westchester District Attorney's office as well as organized crime does. It is absolutely ridiculous that the chief law enforcement officer of Westchester County is also the wife of Al Pirro, convicted federal tax felon, but more importantly *Mr. Fixit.* It is truly a sad testimonial to the level of morality amongst people in high places both in business and in government in and around Westchester County that such a sham should not only be tolerated, but also applauded and encouraged.

Prior to his conviction it was generally acknowledged in the real estate and construction industry that any major project in Westchester had to involve something "under the table" for Al Pirro, especially projects which might encounter some resistance. Al could grease the necessary wheels – for a fee. Even "the Donald," (Trump) discovered he had to pay tribute to the "fix-it man," if he wanted to do business in Westchester.

And, fix it he would. Al Pirro could always find some official, some planner, greedy and corruptible enough to take a bribe, to put in the 'fix'. Al Pirro never saw a proposal that he couldn't turn into 'cash under the table.' He even managed to screw his partners in crime, as came out at the trial where he would double-bill or add on to bills for services unlawfully performed, or unlawfully charged to corporate accounts in the first place.

Was he brazen and careless at times? Yes, perhaps more often than not. He could pretty much do as he pleased. He was the husband of the DA and not only would she not prosecute him or his associates, she had a personal stake in his unlawful and unethical dealings. She was, and still is, his partner in crime, white-collar crime. The $138,000 annual salary she earns as DA is but the tiniest fraction of what it takes to support her and her family's lavish lifestyle.

They are Westchester's "power couple", so described in magazine and newspaper puff articles. Some power. He with the power to commit the bribe, the fraud, and she with the power not to expose or prosecute. That's power, all right! The perfect marriage of corruption and greed— he provides the cash, and she the cover.

There is an old bromide that states, "power corrupts and absolute power corrupts absolutely." How perfectly befitting Westchester's power couple – Jeanine and Al. He has the power to commit crime, and she has the power to condone it. You can't get more absolute than that.

It is apparent that Jeanine is so accustomed to the benefits and comforts provided by white collar crime that she tends not to see it in the light most of us do. Why else does her office almost totally avoid the prosecution of organized crime? Jeanine and Al's connection with organized crime figures was well established more than fifteen years ago when she was forced to withdraw from consideration in the race for Lieutenant Governor because of his connection to criminal elements in the waste hauling industry.

Simply stated, in eight years in office, Jeanine Pirro has turned virtually a "blind eye" toward the operations of organized crime in Westchester. She apparently sees no price-fixing or excesses in the carting of bio-hazardous waste or other garbage, no loan-sharking, no extortion or muscling of small business, no insurance or consumer fraud, no union pension fund problems, no alcohol or tobacco tax scams. In short, organized crime would continue to enjoy a 'field day' in Westchester were it not for the United States Attorney's Office and State Attorney General Eliot Spitzer's vigorous efforts.

Jeanine's concept of organized crime is the operation of your neighborhood bookie. She refers to such arrests as "vital to denying bread and butter to the mob." In truth, under her watch, organized crime has little to fear. After all, how different are mob extortion activities from her husband's lobbying activities with agencies such as the Westchester County Medical Center? A shakedown is a shakedown.

Why should the Westchester County Medical Center be willing to pay Al $200,000 per year as a lobbyist, other than the fact that his wife happens to be the DA? Could there be some connection between retaining Al and the fact that the Medical Center, within six months, was the site of the extraordinary death of a six-year-old in their MRI, plus the loss of two lives and the putting of another in a coma caused by lack of infection control, none of which caused Jeanine to launch a full-scale investigation into possible criminal negligence.

It would appear the hospital really got its money's worth, and Al didn't have to go far to lobby for its interests. But what about the victims? What about the people of Westchester County whose rights to protection from unnecessary injury and illness as well as criminal negligence are compromised by a district attorney and her convicted felon of a lobbyist husband whose household is enriched by $200,000 annually?

As the saying goes, "truth is often expressed in jest." Al Pirro approached the Mayor of the City of New Rochelle, Tim

Idoni, shortly after Al's release from federal prison. Al was looking for lobbying business. He said to the Mayor, who is a strong Democratic leader and a decided supporter of Tony Castro, "You did quite a job on my wife in New Rochelle," referring to how well Tony had done in the election in New Rochelle.

When Idoni responded that he had no business for him, Al cracked, "I understand Jeanine has an indictment for you – only kidding." Before his conviction, he wouldn't have been kidding!

The real questions concerning Al Pirro and his lobbying business are ones that the Westchester community needs to address. The simple fact is that no spouse of the Westchester DA has any ethical or moral right to be soliciting lobbying accounts from any business or institution located in, or doing business in Westchester County. The conflict of interest in such arrangements is both appalling and obvious. No business or institution should fear, or conversely, feel safe from criminal prosecution based upon whether or not they do business with the prosecutor's spouse!

However, in the case of Al Pirro, "Mr. Fixit", the proposition is really a no-brainer. There are many who question what logic there is in having a convicted felon – any convicted felon – acting as a lobbyist at all. After all, a lobbyist is a person who talks to lawmakers and government regulators and administrators about "what they should or should not be doing." Why bother to license and regulate lobbyists at all, if in fact, a convicted felon is permitted to continue practicing and influencing government?

Is it only a coincidence that Jeanine Pirro prosecutes virtually no organized crime activity in Westchester . . . activity which in great measure involves the construction industry, and the fact that the overwhelming majority of her biggest corporate campaign contributions come from the construction industry? Does one conclude that every one of dozens of construction industry corporate contributors to Jeanine Pirro's three campaigns for District Attorney are tied to organized crime or engaged in some criminal enterprise? Certainly not. But does one conclude that there is something about being in the construction industry that makes one more public spirited and generous in support of the campaign of any District Attorney? Certainly not.

Mike Edelman, her husband's former law partner and a Cabal spokesperson, would likely point out that the disproportionate generosity of construction industry contributions to Jeanine's campaign probably stems from their connections to Al and his activities on their behalf over the years. Of course, knowing the nature of "Mr. Fixit's" activities does not make one feel too good about any business which feels obligated to support Al's wife. Worse yet, it doesn't make one feel too comfortable knowing that she welcomes, and survives in office on such support.

It is not as though mob ties and mob activities in Westchester have gone unnoticed and unprosecuted. In September of 2000, headlines in major newspapers proclaimed that "Mob Ties Persist Locally" in Westchester. Indictments charging bid rigging, larceny, racketeering and bribery in construction projects in Westchester and the surrounding area were handed up by federal and state prosecutors as Jeanine's office stood silent.

In one case, Lucchese family members were charged with bribery of an insurance official in connection with the construction of the Doral Arrowood Conference Center. The Arrowood is one of Westchester's largest hotels, with more than 400 rooms. Another member of the so-called "construction panel" was charged with promoting a labor scheme at several construction sites in

Westchester and elsewhere, which generated a "mob-tax" of 5 percent or more of each project's cost.

Again in December 2001, the U.S. Attorney's Office for the Southern District of New York, under Mary Jo White, the same office which had successfully prosecuted Al Pirro eighteen months earlier, announced the indictment of dozens of members of the Genovese crime family for criminal activities in Westchester and elsewhere. Those activities included labor racketeering; extortion, mortgage and insurance fraud, embezzlement, bank fraud, and other construction industry related crimes. Jeanine Pirro's office was still silent!

While Jeanine has "seen no evil, heard no evil" from organized crime operating in Westchester, Mary Jo White and Eliot Spitzer thankfully have. Robert Morganthau, DA of New York County, Manhattan, surely has, too, and continues to investigate and prosecute organized crime activity in his jurisdiction.

By her unwillingness and inability to investigate and prosecute organized crime, Mrs. Pirro raises serious questions as to her fitness to hold office. The people of Westchester County must not be compromised by Jeanine's conflicts of interest and failure to perform her sworn duties.

Whenever questioned about her total lack of organized crime investigation and prosecution, Jeanine Pirro repeatedly points to her six-year-long investigation and conviction in the Louis Balancio killing. But, as anyone who followed that case knows, Balancio's death came as the result of a clash between young hoodlums. It was a bar room brawl between ethnic gang members, which spilled out onto the street and involved 30 gang members, and others who happened to be in the wrong place at the wrong time.

I do not presume to know how, or by whom, Louis Balancio was killed in the early morning hours of February 4, 1994. I do know, however, that the Balancio case was not an organized crime prosecution. It was not a mob rub out, and did not involve "made members" of any crime family or cartel in the act of performing, promoting, or protecting any ongoing criminal enterprise. It was a gang related violent episode with ethnic overtones which may, or may not, have erupted spontaneously.[14]

Whatever else it was, it was a classic Jeanine Pirro theatrical prosecution. Not unlike the Wedra trial, Jeanine, short on evidence, attempted to get a conviction with press releases; sensational, if irrelevant, exhibits; numerous personal courtroom appearances; and the theory of 'guilt by association' with those from whom she accepted a plea. She made no fewer than five personal appearances at the trial, with ten assistant DA's and investigators present as well, in her all-out effort to influence the jury.

Jeanine Pirro desperately needed a conviction in the Balancio case. The case had been hanging fire for more than six years, the killing having occurred just one month after she took office as DA. Most importantly, her husband, Al, had been convicted on all counts by a jury in Federal Court in White Plains just four months earlier, and most observers believed her credibility and her political career were in serious doubt.

The pretrial hype and the conduct of the trial were nothing short of a "full court press" to restore her public image. Not one witness could testify that they actually saw Anthony DiSimone stab or make any contact with the victim. In fact, the entire prosecution case was built around the testimony of Darin Mazzarella, a member of the so-called "Tanglewood Boys" gang whom Jeanine had originally charged with the killing, and who still faced charges in a killing two years earlier, along with other violent crimes.

For his testimony that Anthony DiSimone had told him "he thought he had stabbed an Albanian," - testimony Judge James Cowhey, a long time ally of Jeanine, allowed in as an "exception" to the Hearsay Rule, Mazzarella was cleared of all charges in the case and given a free pass into the Witness Protection Program. Mazzarella, who was up to his ears in other criminal charges unrelated to the Balancio killing, had even agreed to wear a wire to help implicate other members of his gang. He told the jury that he "was in the fight, but did not see the stabbing."

For her part, Jeanine used every trick in the book including the withholding of exculpatory evidence from the defense that a member of the Albanian gang might have committed the killing, until eleven days into the trial. She also had help in her theatrical production. She had help big-time from *The Journal News.* Gary Sherlock's newspaper served, not only for years before and during the trial, as Jeanine's propaganda and publicity agent, but even afterward. Nearly two months following Anthony DiSimone's conviction, on December 13, 2000, there appeared an editorial calling for the stiffest possible sentence, but more significantly, heaping shovel after shovel of praise upon Pirro for her "perseverance" and for having "remained in the trenches."

With all due respect to the Balancio family and their tragic loss, they, too, were sucked into the Jeanine Machine's manipulations and contortions, all striving hard to restore Jeanine's image following her husband's conviction just a few months earlier. Photos of Jeanine consoling Dorothy Balancio, the victim's mother, photos of the family at Louis' gravesite, and other privacy invasive experiences to which the victim's parents, family and friends were all subjected, before, during, and after the trial, were all calculated to bolster Jeanine's damaged public image.

Jeanine Pirro, District Attorney of Westchester County simply does not prosecute organized crime. The Balancio case was not organized crime despite her repeated attempts to characterize it as such. In the 18 months since the Balancio trial she has consistently continued to avoid prosecuting organized crime. One is compelled to conclude, given the realities, the ongoing investigations and prosecutions of organized crime within Westchester by both the United States Attorney and the State Attorney General, that Jeanine's failure is both intentional and purposeful.

One is also compelled to conclude that as between Jeanine and Al, and Al and the business community of Westchester, that since his emergence from prison it's business as usual. Revelations in March and April of 2002 regarding the placement of Al Pirro's former employees and legal representatives in County jobs, as well as Anthony Mangone's with lawyers and tenants of Al Pirro are clear examples of why the District Attorney ought not be the spouse of a convicted felon. All of Jeanine's protestations of ignorance, when confronted with these 'payoff job placements,' are as convincing as her claim of ignorance of their joint ten-year tax fraud.

Their lives and their deeds are inseparable, not merely as husband and wife, but more importantly as co-conspirators. In truth, Jeanine could no more be expected to prosecute organized crime effectively than Al could!

||| Seven |||

The Campaign Of 2001

The Big Lie: "Al Did It All."

Once the dust from the tax fraud trial had settled and the questions, obvious questions, raised in *The New York Times* June 22, 2000 editorial were permitted to go unanswered, Jeanine and her spinsters, Sarah Gaffney Mahoney, Ann Marie Corbalis and others began to float the notion that Jeanine would run for a third term. Their strategy was to blame it all on Al, just as Al had tried to blame it all on his brother Anthony. All they would need to do was to neutralize the Democrats by cutting a deal with Andy Spano and avoiding any direct confrontation with an opposing candidate, or the press. With only one daily newspaper published in Westchester County, *The Journal News,* her task must have appeared easy because her old friend Andy was already under her control.

By Spring of 2001, as if to scare off any potential serious Democratic challenger, the Jeanine Machine published a full-page ad in *The Journal News*, featuring several so-called Democratic supporters of hers. Extolling her "virtues" as District Attorney were such has-beens as former Mayor Ed Koch, Mayor of Mt. Vernon Ernie Davis, and Geraldine Ferraro. Of course, Geraldine, a former prosecutor herself and also another self-righteous wife of a convicted felon and former attorney with mob ties, could be expected to identify with Jeanine.

Money talks and so it didn't hurt her one bit to spend more than $18,000 on that full-page ad. Money was certainly no object, given the hundreds of thousands of dollars that continued to flow in after her reelection in 1997, mostly from corporate and wealthy individual contributors.

Al had helped set the stage for Jeanine's "blame it all on Al" victim strategy as early as December 2000, about four weeks before surrendering to authorities to serve a sentence that was supposed to be 29 months but turned out to be only 11. On December 13, he went to *New York Post* columnist Cindy Adams, big time propagandist for Jeanine. Al told her "the best thing for Jeanine would be to divorce me, but she won't make the move, and I love her too much to leave her and free her up. I'm just not man enough." The following day *The Journal News* repeated his remarks.

Then there was District Attorney Newsletter Vol. 1 No. 4, Winter 2001, which was mailed to 365,000 Westchester households, at a cost of approximately $150,000 – printing, postage and handling, all at taxpayer's expense, and, as usual, all about Jeanine. Containing no fewer than four pictures of her, each and every article, with the single exception of an obituary for a former Assistant D.A., was an article about Jeanine. One article on the front page included a quote. Jeanine Pirro said: "DNA identification is the finger of God pointing to the criminal." What an interesting quote coming from a woman who gave two of her investigators to her husband to try to discredit and undermine the paternity and child support case of his girlfriend, Jessica Marciano, for their illegitimate 16 year-old daughter, given that DNA proved ultimately that he was the father!

Who in Westchester could have been startled to see her puffing and blowing her own horn once again, striking up that all too familiar pose with her arms crossed in front of her. Those who study body language tell us that stance is highly defensive and withholding. What a surprise!

Bugging the Democrats

On the heels of what she had done to my client and the conviction of her husband which would have prompted a resignation from anyone with an ounce of scruples, Jeanine's announced intention to run again coupled with the firing up of her "Machine" was more than I was willing to stand still for. March was fast approaching and I knew that within 90 days or less, candidates would be nominated for county and local elections.

I located and called the Westchester County Democratic Committee office and reached a woman who identified herself as "Rocky", the Director of Finance and Operations. I got right to the point. "Have the Democrats in this county decided on a candidate for DA yet?" Her response was not too encouraging and left me with the feeling that nobody else felt as strongly about not reelecting Mrs. Pirro as I did.

I called a second time and told Rocky that I was going to be speaking to someone I thought was eminently qualified and whom I would try to persuade to run. I hung up with her and called Ben Gershman, inviting him to lunch the next afternoon. I gave no clue as to my intention, preferring to lay the idea on him in person.

We met for lunch the next day. I wasted no time telling him how it would be wonderful if he would consider running against Jeanine Pirro. I covered all of the obvious reasons why he was the one to do it – his 12 years with Manhattan DA Frank Hogan, his authorship of *Prosecutorial Misconduct*, his professorship at Pace University Law School, and his close monitoring of her office and her behavior and commentaries in the press.

Perhaps because I was one of his favorite former law students, Ben was patient with me, even a bit flattered by my belief in him and my enthusiasm. But I really hadn't lit a fire under him. He informed me that he had run unsuccessfully as a Democrat for local legislator some years earlier and it didn't appear that it was a pleasurable experience for him. Still, he promised to consider it.

In the days that followed, I stayed in touch with Ben, even faxed him a piece that I had written, "Wake Up Westchester." He liked it so well, he said he would have given me an "A" in Con-Law for it. I told him it was but a sample of what I would write for him if he ran against Jeanine. He remained non-committal.

I stayed in touch over the next several weeks with Rocky, calling about every 2 weeks or so to check whether any potential candidate had surfaced. I even went so far as to attend a $150 per plate dinner which I really couldn't afford, on the possibility that I might press my mission to awaken the Democrats to the need of running someone against Jeanine.

Finally, about mid-May, there was talk in the press. Mark Oxman, the Executive Director of the Westchester Democratic Committee and sometimes spokesperson, was indicating that the Democrats would soon be producing a candidate in time for their nominating convention about 10 days away. William Aaronwald, a former Assistant US Attorney and an occasional critic of Jeanine was mentioned in *The Journal News* and on cable news as a possible contender.

Meeting the Candidate

As the convention drew within a few days, a new name was added to a very short list – Tony Castro. I called Rocky once again and asked her to please put whoever got the nomination for DA in touch with me. I wanted to help any genuine candidate who might emerge in any way that I could.

My first contact with Tony Castro was by telephone a day

or so before the Party Convention. I felt immediately comfortable with his tone and apparent sincerity. I suggested we meet for lunch so that I might get to know him and he might assess whether or not I could be of value to his campaign if it turned out that he got the nomination. I would bring some samples of my writing.

As it turned out, we met for dinner after work. Tony was employed as Deputy Bureau Chief for Homicides and the Grand Jury at the Bronx DA's Office, and dinner at 6:00 PM worked fine for both of us. It was May 30th, just six days since he had received the nod.

We enjoyed about two hours of getting to know each other and discussing the adversary over dinner. I liked what he had to say. He had an old-fashioned quality about him – youthful, but not slick, at 45 years. His speech did not betray the fact that he had come to this country at the age of nine from Portugal, not speaking a word of English, or that he had grown up in New Bedford, Massachusetts.

It was obvious that we shared at least one common interest – defeating Jeanine Pirro in her attempt for a third term as DA, and that we could probably work well together towards that objective. He seemed to have both the depth of experience to handle the office as well as the people skills and youthful good looks to be an appealing candidate.

<u>One Foot in the Boat</u>

For the next few weeks, I kept in touch with Tony about every three or four days. He was attempting to get things in order at work, hoping to approach Bronx DA Robert Johnson with 30 days notice before resigning to devote full time to the campaign. However, Jeanine had already gotten to Johnson, a Democrat, who by rights should have been proud of Tony's having been nominated.

Instead, when Tony approached him, offering 30 days notice, Johnson replied, through a henchman, "that won't be necessary, you can leave in three days!"

Over the years, I had come to recognize that Robert Johnson left a great deal to be desired both as a prosecutor and as a public figure. He was no Mario Merola! Given the way he willingly did Jeanine's bidding, it was obvious he wasn't much of a man, either .

About three weeks following our first encounter, I invited both Tony and Professor Gershman to lunch, promising each that I would mostly eat while they got acquainted. It was a good meeting. Ben was favorably impressed with the candidate for all of the reasons I had been, as well as for what one great prosecutor might see in another.

As summer arrived, I found myself spending lunch hours and time after work at Democratic Headquarters. Because Andy Spano had established his own headquarters (staffed with several paid assistants who normally held County-paid positions within his office), and Lisa Copeland was operating out of Mt. Vernon in her bid for County Clerk,[15] David Alpert, Chairman of the Democratic County Committee, graciously offered space to "Castro and Company" at Democratic Headquarters.

The "Rag Tag Volunteers" as Tony fondly referred to them, consisted of the following: Ben and Jonathan (two guys I was always tempted to call Ben and Jerry) who did research and investigation, attended functions with Tony, and generally assisted and shared ideas with him; Rocky, who appeared to come with the office, but did so much more; and a half-dozen women who had worked hard for Hillary the year before.

Tony was confronting a tough task. He was virtually unknown, with few, if any, contacts to big contributors. His opponent had both facial and name recognition, even if she was not always favorably thought of. She would likely have a million dollars to spend. Tony was hoping to raise about $200,000.

She had other things going for her, as we would discover. Tony had the Portuguese-American community with five clubs in Westchester,[16] little political experience, but big hearts and a desire to help this son of Portugal. Suddenly, there were Portuguese everywhere. Tony estimated perhaps 50,000 in Westchester, mostly quiet, hard working and non-political.

The first fund raiser was held at the Portuguese-American Club in Tarrytown on July 14th. Fewer than 100 supporters showed up but it was a successful function. Many who came were from the Bronx DA's office, young attorneys in their 30's who had worked under Tony and had loved him. One couple, who had both worked for Tony - Dave and Renee Godosky - were both sincere and generous with their time, their ideas and their financial support.

I came away from this first function impressed with two things I had witnessed. First, people who had worked for him in the difficult environment of the Bronx DA's office loved him, both men and women alike. Second, when Tony rose to his feet to address the crowd, he was sincere and convincing, if a little nervous – but clearly a leader.

There was another thing that was memorable about that first fundraiser. I got to meet Tony's wife, Rose, and their two children, Anthony and Isabel. I was immediately comfortable with Rose, a former real estate attorney. She was warm and down-to-earth and loved being a mom. The kids were adorable. I wondered to myself if Rose had any idea just how hectic things would become.

To my surprise and delight, the evening raised $6,000. People really cared for this man. They knew that every dollar would be put to good use.

Coming on Board as Director

Following the Tarrytown fundraiser, I found myself feeling closer to the candidate and his family. I was becoming as motivated to see Tony serve as District Attorney as I was to see Mrs. Pirro removed. Others were already hard at work trying to make my wishes reality.

Ben, a high school teacher in Brooklyn, with a family history in politics, and Jonathan who would be returning to graduate study in the fall, had been busy amassing newspaper clippings and election statistics from Jeanine's two prior campaigns. They also answered calls and helped Tony in every way they could. The women volunteers, collectively known as the Westchester Democratic Action Coalition, worked on Tony's appearances and events calendar, handled bookkeeping and correspondence, as well as contacting associates for fundraisers and volunteer assignments. They had worked hard to help elect Hillary with little in the way of gratitude for their efforts. Tony was different. Everyone had access to him. You couldn't help feeling his gratitude and humility.

It was late July and there was so much that would have to get done. Tony had officially been a candidate for two months, and nobody on the street knew who he was. Jeanine knew who he was and she didn't like it. She knew from the moment of his acceptance statement that Tony Castro was not about to "throw the fight." She would do everything possible to try to discredit him.

Word got back to Tony within days of his nomination that calls were coming into the Bronx DA's office from Jeanine's office attempting to get some dirt on him. Tony had trained hundreds of young DA's over the years and it must have been very frustrating to Jeanine not to find one who had one bad thing to say about him. Finally, in desperation, she began to spread a lie (nothing unusual for Jeanine) amongst law enforcement in the County that he was a prosecutor of police.

Nothing could have been further from the truth. It happened that in his fourteen years as a prosecutor in the Bronx, he never had the occasion to prosecute a rogue cop. More importantly, as I would discover on the campaign trail, as we frequently bumped into detectives from the NYPD who lived in Westchester, the police who knew Tony and had worked cases with him couldn't rave enough about him.

Detectives would stop us on the street and in restaurants and would go on about what a great guy Tony was, how he helped them with their cases and never tried to take credit or upstage their investigations. I couldn't help thinking on those occasions how grateful those police officers in Westchester would be to get "media hound" Jeanine Pirro out of their way. After all, it would be a long time before police departments in Westchester would forget the hostage situation in Eastchester in which Officer Michael Frey was gunned down. They would not soon forget how Jeanine thoughtlessly opened her mouth on live TV, for everyone including the gunman to hear, that she would seek the death penalty, thereby placing the hostage and all at the scene at greater risk. In fact, she never did seek it.

Jeanine was beginning to become upset. She had been promised a pushover and Castro was no pushover. What was even more threatening to her throne was his announced intention to make her role in the 10-year tax fraud and other relevant misbehavior of hers issues for discussion in the campaign.

I was taking the last couple of days in July and the first few of

August for a needed vacation trip to California. As excited as I was to be getting away, as the plane left the runway, I was pulling index cards from my pocket to jot down things I felt I needed to do for Tony as soon as I got back.

Before we landed in San Diego, I had decided that I had to leave my job and work full-time for the campaign. I had stood for public office four times myself, but never against the likes of Jeanine Pirro. Tony would need all the help I could possibly give him and all the help he could possibly get.

Two days after returning from California I sent Tony a memorandum. (See pages 86-89)

MEMORANDUM

TO: TONY

FROM: RICHARD

DATE: AUGUST 7, 2001

RE: A RAFT OF IDEAS, ISSUES, AND CONCERNS

Issues To Drive Home

1. Mrs. Pirro is no longer effective because:

She compromised her integrity by passively and actively participating in the Federal Tax Fraud for which her husband is now serving 29 months in a federal prison. She is, in fact, an unindicted co-conspirator!

She knowingly and intentionally enjoys a lavish lifestyle from the fruits of her husband's criminal activities over many years, conduct which went far beyond mere tax fraud and income tax evasion, conduct which touched communities all over Westchester as he used his influence as the husband of the District Attorney to install his contractors in many public projects who would then funnel huge kickbacks, for purposes of bribery, back to him.

Case in Point The Peekskill Hospital Expansion Project which cost the hospital, and the community which labored for years to raise the funds, $550,000-more than it should have because Al Pirro and Rober Boyle split that money as kickback and bribery.

She selectively prosecutes, as demonstrated by her failure to prosecute her husband and his associates for the Peekskill Hospital scheme, thus allowing the statute of limations to run out.

2. Mrs. Pirro is a politically ambitious office seeker who is driven by her lust for power and position, and who now seeks to cleanse herself by re-election to a position she clearly has betrayed. That's cleanse as in "out, out dammed spot."

3. Mrs. Pirro has betrayed the Public Trust by allowing her husband to criminally trade on her position as District Attorney while she continued to turn a "blind eye" to his activities, in fact, benefitting and enjoying the fruits of that activity in her lavish celebrity-like life at public expense.

4. Mrs. Pirro further betrayed the Public Trust by actively participating in her husband's and her tax fraud, not merely by signing their fradulent tax returns for more than ten years, but also by engaging in deceptive maneuvers as when she pretended to aquire a car loan for her expensive Mercedes, which Al immediately paid off illegally with corporate funds.

5. Mrs. Pirro's career in public life has been forever tainted by her knowing acceptance of, and participation in, her husband's criminal activity, and more importantly, by her refusal to expose and prosecute those activities as she surely would have had she not been the beneficiary and co-conspirator that she was and still is!

6. Despite all of her high-profile, publicity seeking activity Mrs. Pirro will forever be "damaged goods."

7. Mrs. Pirro operates the Distict Attorney's office by a double standard, one for herself and her powerful friends, and another for the rest of us!

Jeanine Pirro, Myth vs Reality

We are dealing with a larger-than-life persona in Mrs. Pirro. And, much like an over-ripened apple, she is still pretty shiny on the outside, but rotten to the core on the inside! She knows she stinks, and she knows we know she stinks. As a result she is very vulnerable and nervous. Her body language is very revealing.

Furthermore, she knows in her "heart of hearts," that she does not deserve to be Dog Catcher, much less the Chief Law Enforcement Officer of the County, and her guilt will be her undoing if we simply begin immediately to hammer away at her misdeeds, day after day, from every angle, relentlessly. Never mind the *politically correct idiots* who say we should not be negative! There is simply no way around the facts as they are, and there is no need to be "tiptoeing" around this vindictive cirminal individual. Remember, in her desperation to hold onto power she will stop at nothing to destroy you or anyone who might oppose her. She has lived the life, danced to the music, and now she "must pay the piper."

Mrs. Pirro just as so many persons who have taken pleasure in meting out a pain, can not take the pain herself , in this case *the painful truth.* She will continue to put up a good front unless, and until we begin to hammer her relentlessly and hammer her we must. She has let the people of Westchester down. We must not do the same!

To get moving On

<u>You must immediately have an undeniable presence.</u> We must call for and request debating opportunities from:

Pace University Law School, (ask for a series of three debates at Moot Court)

Channel 12 Cable News Network (ask for two debates)

League of Women Voters (ask for Candidates' Night Interviews)

Village and Town Taxpayers and Civic Association candidate interviews.

Major Newspaper Endorsement Question Forums.

We must generate a flood of "letters to the editor" to not only *The Journal News*, but also to the major NYC papers as well as the local ethnic, village and town papers, particularly the Latino press!

We must design and quickly obtain campaign buttons and literature. We need these yesterday! **TONY CASTRO**, the name and the face must be everywhere, immediately, if not sooner.

Your message to women, to people of color, to people of conscience, to people of courage, must begin to circulate now. Your positive message must certainly get out there, while at the same time we continue to reveal and expose her misdeeds and her shortcomings. It must be a two-pronged approach, and one must not preclude the other.

A week before leaving on vacation, I had sat in as Tony interviewed Joe Rifkin, a campaign strategist who would create mailers and help plan strategy. Joe was based about an hour away in Orange County and was working for several other candidates in other counties. He would not be a much needed campaign director. Ben would soon be returning to his teaching responsibilities and Jonathan to school. Nancy, although a leader of the Coalition, was employed and clearly could not invest the time a full-time director would have to devote. Beside, nobody else on board had ever been through the process before. Tony required someone who would be where and when he was needed, and someone who could produce a press release on a moment's notice.

I offered myself, knowing better than anyone what lay ahead. By process of elimination, I became the Campaign Director. I didn't need all that much sleep anyway. I now had both feet in the boat.

While I was away, Tony had attended the Arab-American Day Festival in Yonkers. Seeing him there enraged Jeanine, causing her to make a hollering declaration from the platform that she was "the only one who is 100% like you." Tony got a good taste of her pomposity and the extremes to which she would go to keep the office. That she would tell people, in effect, "vote for me, because I am an Arab like you" was very offensive, I felt.

Ten days into August and Tony had raised about $20,000 and was justifiably proud of his achievement. He was becoming a first-rate telemarketing fundraiser for political charity – and he was the charity! Not every candidate who stands for public office can handle direct solicitation of financial assistance from supporters. With each passing day, Tony got better and better at it. All the same, one of the volunteers, Jane M. appointed herself as his fundraising monitor seeing to it that if he was in the office, he would make three or more hours of phone calls, attempting to raise at least $1,000 or more per day. I was amazed by the number of lists of people the volunteers, Rocky and Tony himself produced to work from. Twenty thousand quickly became forty and then sixty.

We were all very conscious of the need to raise as much money as we possibly could. We couldn't hope to come anywhere near the kind of bankroll Jeanine brought into the race, much less what she would continue to receive. Her filings with the Board of Elections in the 1993 campaign and 1997 campaign and beyond were filled with dozens and dozens of $5,000 corporate contributors. And equal numbers of generous, or perhaps, *concerned* individuals.

The campaign finance laws allowed a maximum contribution from a corporation not to exceed $5,000, and from an individual, $25,000 in this race. Jeanine was not the only big bucks fundraising candidate running for county-wide office. There was, of course, Andy Spano, her Democratic counterpart in the "big fix". It was rumored, even early in the campaign, that Andy had about $2 million to spend but that was understandable given two facts.

As incumbent County Executive, it was natural to expect Andy Spano, who controlled a great amount of patronage and appointments, not to mention contracts with the County, to draw big bucks. In effect, vendors and office and favor-seekers, would naturally curry favor with the person they believed they would need to do business with after the election. But what about Jeanine?

What could Jeanine Pirro do for businesses, especially the construction and contracting business, that so many were so anxious to contribute maximum donations to her reelection effort? Could it be that what motivated many of her big givers was precisely the opposite of what motivated Andy's? Could it be that in Jeanine's case they were trying to <u>avoid</u> doing business with her office – official business?

Those were questions that certainly occurred to me and certainly to others, but 90 days or less from Election Day we needed to spend our time in more positive pursuits. There were, however, a few straight-out violations, one of which Ben and Jonathan had found, and one that I found in her 1997 filings. Ticketmaster, clearly a corporation, had contributed $10,868.30 to Jeanine's 1997 campaign, on September 29, 1997, with check number 34076. That figure was more than double the legally allowable limit.

I personally pursued the Ticketmaster check because it occurred to me that the figure was unusual and the source was easily accessible and some accountability might reasonably be expected. We did not go running to the media as Jeanine did when she inadvertently received an invitation at her office to one of Tony's fundraisers.[17]

Although the check had been sent from Ticketmaster's office on W. 57th Street, in New York City, the corporation counsel I wound up dealing with was in Los Angeles. I faxed and forwarded the following letter to their Spokesperson, Mr. Larry Solters. Apparently, Jeanine was not the only one who needed spokespersons to spin explanations for inappropriate conduct.

More than two weeks passed without a response. I then made a number of phone calls over the next two weeks. Each time I was offered some excuse as to why Mr. Solters, the *spokesperson* would not speak to me. Finally, when it became obvious to everyone in his office that I was not going away, they put me in touch with their legal department and an attorney named Ed Weiss. It

FRIENDS OF TONY CASTRO
170 EAST POST ROAD, SUITE 210
WHITE PLAINS NY 10601
914.946.2236

August 23, 2001

Mr. Larry Solters, Spokesperson
Ticketmaster
3701 Wilshire Boulevard, 6th Floor
Los Angeles, CA 90010

By fax: 213.639.3950

Dear Mr. Solters,

Upon examination of records from the New York State Board of Elections, we came across a political donation that was made to "Friends of Jeanine Pirro" at Franklin Avenue, White Plains, NY 10601, received September 29, 1997. Records indicate the donor was "Ticketmaster" at 555 West 57th Street, New York, NY 10019. The check number was #34076, in the amount of $10,868.30.

Obviously, this entry caught our attention, both for the unusual amount and the total sum.

We would appreciate explicit information regarding the following:

1- The title of the account upon which the check was drawn.
2- The individual or individuals who signed the check.
3- The date of the check.
4- The name of the bank and bank address from which the check was drawn.
5- The specific purpose for which the check was made.

I wish to thank you for your prompt response and cooperation in this matter.

Yours very truly,

Richard Blassberg
Campaign Director

was obvious to me that there was no legally acceptable reason for their abuse of the election law, and they were merely stalling for time, having surely communicated with Jeanine's people.

Ed Weiss, a bit quivering at first, attempted to explain that the money wasn't a contribution in the usual sense, but rather a percentage of proceeds from some event handled by Ticketmaster to fund Pirro's campaign. He acknowledged that it was, in fact, a corporate check. The long and the short of it was that Jeanine had made an arrangement with a corporation that she knew would result in an illegal corporate contribution to her campaign and it did, in fact, result in one.

Mr. Weiss promised to forward a correspondence acknowledging our conversation and explaining the circumstances of the unlawful contribution. The letter was never sent. We did not go to the press as we felt that there were more fundamental and meaningful issues regarding Jeanine and the conduct of her office that needed our attention. Furthermore, if we had really wanted to explore her list of contributors from whom she had accepted large sums of money, (that a morally and ethically sound DA would have returned), we could go on forever.

By contrast, about ten days after my last conversation with Mr. Weiss, Tony received a call from a reporter for *The Journal News* questioning an entry in our most recent filing with the Board of Elections. The question involved, as luck would have it, the largest contribution we had received. It was from a wealthy woman in California who was a close friend of one of our supporters and advisors, a former Assistant United States Attorney. The check was for $10,000 and naturally stood out immediately amongst hundreds of grassroots contributions of $50, $100, $200 and the like.

The problem with the check had nothing to do with the

sum. It had to do with the spouse of the woman who signed it. He had pled guilty to insider trading, a violation of SEC rules, and had served his sentence in federal detention. What made matters appear worse, was that the checking account from which the check was drawn bore both of their names. Tony was at once confronted with a dilemma, and the first crisis of his campaign. He had not known the nature of the contributor's husband's legal problems. Clearly, the contribution was well within legal limits and coming from someone three thousand miles away was not likely intended to curry favor or special treatment from the Westchester District Attorney's Office should Tony be elected.

At this point, $10,000 represented about 20 percent of all we had left in the account. There were many advisors who implored Tony not to return the money because it was perfectly legal and ethical. Tony himself observed "if it is wrong for the wife of a convicted felon to contribute to my campaign, is it right for the wife of a convicted felon, such as Mrs. Pirro, to accept money to her campaign or to contribute money to the campaigns of others."

I, for one, could see the merit in each argument. My advice was simply to do what his instincts told him was right for him. He wasted no time doing just that. Within twenty-four hours, he decided that even the mere appearance of impropriety was unacceptable for someone seeking an office of such high public trust and that he must regretfully return the check.

Tony's decision caught Jeanine and her people totally off guard. One of them, Sara Gaffney Mahoney, her chief strategist, was quoted in the newspaper, "even when he does something wrong, it comes out right." For weeks afterward, our pride in our candidate was further bolstered by the fact that he had probably gotten $30,000 worth of good publicity for the $10,000 he returned.

The Campaign Picks Up Speed

As we entered the last week of August, with Labor Day almost upon us, the pace of events began to quicken. After much expectation and some prodding from what seemed like a hungry press, we issued our first press release. It was a well researched and documented broadside, carefully timed to appear just two days before Women's Equality Day.

The article, misleadingly headlined by *The Journal News*, "Pirro Hiring Record Assailed" was placed on the first page of the second (Local) section rather than the front page of the paper where it truly belonged. The subheading referred to Tony as "Challenger: DA Keeps Women from Upper Level Jobs."

The piece, which ran about twelve column inches, pointed out the fact that amongst 118 Assistant DA's working for Jeanine, only 40 were woman – and that of those 40, fully 29 were languishing in the two lowest tiers out of eight. It further accurately reported that of 47 attorneys and investigators earning $100,000 or more, only 9 were women. And finally, of 34 criminal investigators, remarkably only two were women.

By comparing Pirro's appalling numbers to those of the Bronx DA where Tony had worked for 14 years, the message was powerful, indeed. In the Bronx, 58 percent of the D.A.s were women and the top four categories were staffed with 31 women and 31 men. The comparison defeated any excuse offered by Jeanine's PR mouthpiece, Ann Marie Corbalis.

The impact of the revelations, timed as they were, absolutely devastated Jeanine. A major Women's Equality Day Event was scheduled for Friday, August 24th at the White Plains Public Library. The event honored Congresswoman Nita Lowey as "Woman of the Year" and other Westchester Women of Accomplishment including Polly Rothstein, founder and retiring President of the Westchester Coalition for Legal Abortion, the most powerful, nonpartisan and politically influential women's organization in Westchester. The article which had appeared on Wednesday, just two days prior, was the talk of the gathering. More significantly, Jeanine Pirro who had been the recipient of the award just a few years earlier, and who always attended this annual affair, failed to show her face.

Tony was warmly received by many at the gathering, including Congresswoman Lowey. He and a number of our volunteers came away from the event feeling encouraged. We were prepared with a follow-up release which would discuss positive steps that Tony intended to take, not only to correct the imbalances in the office, but also to deal with other issues such as family and emergency leave, by initiating a job-sharing program and other innovative ideas if elected. *The Journal News* refused to print them.

Jeanine and her machine could not tolerate such a revelation – such exposure of myth vs. reality. She reached up to the highest authority at *The Journal News* to be certain that such an honest portrayal of the facts concerning her conduct and the conduct of her office would never see print for the rest of the campaign. In fact, the next four press releases, all of which were very positive and constructive, were either totally ignored, buried in some "attack" release of hers, or turned around 180 degrees to state exactly the opposite of what was intended.

Not content to merely freeze Tony Castro out for the balance of the time to election, *The Journal News* twice omitted his name in the caption beneath photos of him with others, and when compelled to acknowledge his existence in any news item from Jeanine or another source, would refuse to mention him by name. It was always "challenger", "foe", "adversary", etc. There could be no question that *The Journal News* was more than biased in Jeanine's favor. They were nothing less than a propaganda arm of her campaign!

We were disturbed but hoped to overcome the great communication gap caused by the "freeze-out" with mailings, debates, possible radio and TV spots, if we could raise enough money in time. It was the first week of September and Tony was raising almost $2000 per day on the phone. We had raised $80,000 and might reach our goal of $200,000 by Election Day.

It was Monday, September 10, 2001 and Tony, Carl B. and I met at the New Rochelle Rail Road station of Metro North to launch our grass-roots appeal to Westchester commuters. Carl, who was the lone male member of the Coaltion of volunteers, and a retired attorney, had already been hard at work for many weeks digesting the transcripts of the tax fraud trial and other materials in an effort to put together a "white paper"[18] regarding Mrs. Pirro's own hands-on culpable conduct. In addition to Carl's work and my own research, we had the information that Ben and Jonathan had gathered, as well as the work of George F., a retired journalist and fine researcher to call upon. George had come forward to assist without any prior connection to the Democratic organization.

There we were, 6:30 AM, armed with a great palm card of Tony, smartly designed by Joe Rifkin. On the front flap, Tony walking alongside a building with columns that gave the appearance of a courthouse, but was actually the back of the White Plains Public Library. (There was no chance we could photograph with the actual County Courthouse, which houses the DA's Office. It was under reconstruction, covered by scaffolding and construction elevator shafts, because some 20 years after construction the surface of the building was falling off because of faulty construction by a contractor brought to the job by none other than *Mr. Fixit*, hubby, Al.)

The back flap had a great picture of Rose and the children with Tony. Inside were the details of his education at Harvard on a soccer scholarship, Boston Law School, and a brilliant 14-year career as an Assistant DA in the Bronx. We made an initial printing of 75,000. Tony looked so great on the front, and the reaction, especially from women was so good, that we blew it up and went with it for our signs. The signs, which looked great in store windows, were a handy width, able to fit neatly into the I-beams at most of the Metro North rail stations.

The plan for the railroads was to cover almost every station on the Hudson, Harlem and New Haven lines – about 50 in all. Carl was a great campaigner, Tony thoroughly enjoyed meeting the public, and I loved it.

As planned we were on the New Rochelle platform by 6:30 AM and greeting and briefly talking to commuters. We worked it for two hours and went for coffee at a local luncheonette. We felt exhilarated and energized by the experience. Commuters had responded well and we had given out about 1700 palm cards. Tomorrow, Tuesday, September 11th, we were scheduled to do Larchmont.

We had mapped out an ambitious schedule of commuter campaigning that would require Tony, Carl and I to be up every weekday morning by 5:30 AM, if not earlier, depending upon which station we were working. Naturally, we would be in dress attire with ties. My blazers were going to get a good workout. It was planned, whenever our volunteers could arrange it, to have local Democratic Committee people and office holders accompany the three of us in their communities where commuters would likely know them.

<u>9/11 HAPPENS!</u>

Things were looking up. We were raising close to $2,000 a day. Tony had gotten the WCLA endorsement, the single most important endorsement in terms of votes. We had kicked off our railroad campaign with a great morning at New Rochelle, and Tony, Carl, and I were spreading out to cover the Larchmont Station on the New Haven line, which had three very busy New York bound entrances.

Tony and Carl were working side by side at the main entry point. I covered the area where cars and buses stopped. It was hectic, but workable.

I tried to be humorous, and still drive home a point. For example, when the next train was just a minute or so down the track, and several commuters were gathered, some reading or glancing at Tony's palmcard, I would say, "Tony's going to bring something different to the D.A.'s Office folks." Then I would pause to get their attention, and say, "Honesty." It always got a lot of smiles and nods of approval.

Tony was a big hand shaker, and the women were especially fond of him. Sometimes when I was working several feet ahead of him, I would embarrass him by telling a cluster of women, as I handed them his palmcard, "He's even better looking than his picture."

What I grew to like best were those moments when the next train was not due for several minutes and I had handed a palmcard to someone who might have made a remark in defense of Jeanine. If it was a woman I might ask, "What is it that you like best about Mrs. Pirro? Do you believe she's a women's advocate?"

Most often they would say, "Yes" and I would go into the revelations about her "glass ceiling." It raised a lot of eyebrows.

If I thought they might be receptive, I would ask, "Do you really believe she didn't know what she was signing for ten years?" She was very vulnerable in so many areas. In September she was up to 38 pedophile convictions and only 3 had done any jail time.

We were informed in late August that Tony had earned the WCLA endorsement, based on integrity. Their endorsement was much sought after because they produce a voter's guide, which many of the 70,000 women on their mailing list in Westchester bring right into the voting booth. However, getting their endorsement was no easy task. It required thoughtfulness and honesty in filling out their thirty- five question "minefield."

Tony had just begun to grapple with it in early August. Ben and Jonathan had reviewed it with him. When I sat down with him a week later, he still had several unresolved issues.

We went over each and every question, some of which might have seemed redundant to the casual reader. Each was designed to deal with a slightly different set of hypothetical circumstances. It was necessary to keep in mind always that the focus of the Coalition was to preserve a woman's right to a legal abortion.

Tony had probably spent more than six hours thoughtfully and carefully answering each question, trying to grasp the subtle difference the organization was attempting to tease out, and discerning the implications for legal abortion. In those instances where his legal duty, if elected District Attorney, to uphold the statutes on the books, conflicted with his personal beliefs, Tony took the time and trouble to cite and explain the intent of the law.

When the WCLA leaders called to inform him that he had won their endorsement, they explained that he had answered their questionnaire 100% correctly. They said they also appreciated the time and effort that he put into explaining the statutes he would be compelled to enforce. They told Tony that Jeanine had left six or more answers blank.

The WCLA was particularly upset with Jeanine Pirro because, even with their assistance she could not answer several of the questions, and seemed uncertain about the law. They confided that she was "hopping mad" when they advised her that Tony would be receiving their endorsement, and that she immediately began to take reprisal against the Coalition's founder and president, Polly Rothstein.[19]

The Larchmont railroad station went very well. We handed out more than 1,300 palmcards greeting as many commuters rushing off to work between 6:30 and 8:30. Carl headed home, and Tony and I went into the village for coffee at Starbucks. At 8:50 I glanced at my watch and suggested we probably should get rolling to the office to get a start on the day's fundraising and writing activities.

The drive to headquarters in White Plains was about 17 minutes or so. As I pulled into the parking lot, John the attendant approached my car and said, "What's the matter, your radio broken?" I couldn't imagine what he was shouting about.

Tony was just pulling in behind me. John waved him around me and said, "Don't you know, an airplane crashed into the World Trade Center?" I turned on my radio as I parked, in time to hear, "A second plane has struck the other tower!" I still remember wondering in that moment, "How many of the people we saw off at the railroad this morning are in those towers?"

Tony and I rushed upstairs to turn on the radio and television. As the enormity of the disaster became quickly apparent, with people leaping to their deaths from more than a thousand feet, the reality gripped us both that some of the 1,300 people we had greeted and given our palmcards to, just a few hours earlier, might never be coming home again.

Like everyone, everywhere, we simply were not prepared to accept what we were witnessing. It had the feeling, those old enough to remember will somehow never forget, that came over us as we watched Jack Ruby kill Lee Harvey Oswald in the basement of Dallas Police Headquarters on November 23, 1963: the feeling "this can't really be happening!"

It was 9-11 and a 911 event such as never before. Nobody in those first few hours could envision the broad scope of the tragedy. Surely all that we were doing; what we had been doing just hours earlier, was swallowed up in the enormity and the sweep of what had just occurred. The implications for our campaign were clearly not upper-most in our minds. Even had we had the presence to assess our drastically altered situation, we were swept too far away by the tidal force of the event to notice or care.

It seemed that Tony and I simultaneously understood, by about 10:30AM, that given the incredible number of people who might have been injured, vast amounts of blood would be needed immediately. A call to the White Plains Hospital revealed that the process was already underway. We arrived at the hospital about 10:50 – exactly two hours after the first terrorist plane had struck, and there were already more than 150 people lined up.

An attorney friend, Rocco D'Agostino, who shared an office with my former employer, was just leaving with his wife as we arrived. They had already given blood. I briefly introduced them to Tony. Rocco and I promised to be in touch. Rocco's dad, Charles D'Agostino Sr., was still practicing at 80, and was a well-known, very active fundraiser and worker for the last four Republican Presidents.

Just seeing all of those people, and those who kept pouring in as we waited, made me feel so good to be alive . . . to be an American. We were running on adrenaline and there was no thought in our minds about how things might be changed forever.

By nightfall, we started to look at our calendar for the next day, the day after, and the days after that. We quickly began to grasp the impact the attack at the World Trade Center was immediately going to have, not only on our little campaign, but on our lives and the lives of everyone we knew and cared about.

Virtually all campaign activity on our part was brought to an immediate halt. No railroad commuter effort, no fundraisers were held, no calling for dollars. In short, all political activity was suspended by our campaign for more than two weeks, and fundraising for more than four weeks. Tony just didn't have the heart to call for money on the heels of our national loss.

We concentrated on planning and writing for the precious weeks that hopefully would lay ahead once things might return to normal. Nobody could say for sure how long it might be before the country would start rolling again. Major league baseball had suspended play. More significantly for us, the hot Democratic primary for Mayor of New York City, and races throughout the State that were held on that morning of September 11th had to be rescheduled. There was even talk of postponing the General Election scheduled for November 6th, less than two months away.

As the persons responsible were identified, and their evil motives based on religious and ethnic division came to light, I couldn't help reflecting on what Jeanine had said just 44 days earlier at the Arab-American festival. Shouting in anger over the presence of Tony Castro, she commanded, "Remember I am the only one who is 100% like you!" That she should seek to divide people by their ethnicity was truly unforgivable. Perhaps only a coincidence, but shortly after Jeanine's angry declaration, a near riot broke out at the festival which required several uniformed police officers to quell.

What greater evidence of her sociopathic personality does one need beyond the fact that having made such an inflammatory statement, Jeanine could then go to synagogues in Harrison and elsewhere to deliver lectures on bias and ethnic-hate-motivated crimes? In a nation composed of immigrants from all over the world, one should be proud of his or her origins and surely Jeanine Ferris Pirro has every right to be proud of her Lebanese ancestry. However, to use ethnicity as a basis by which to suggest someone should elect you over someone else, particularly to a position sworn to uphold the law, is clearly divisive.

About two weeks following the World Trade Center attack, Jeanine, who had been "ducking and dodging" all proposals for a debate with Tony, announced through her mouthpiece, Ms. Mahoney, that she had lost someone at the World Trade Center whom she would not identify, and that she was "suspending all campaign activity indefinitely." My response to Tony after reading it, was "sure." The fact was, in 1997, she debated Joanne Naughton, her Democratic opponent, five times.

We understood Jeanine's unwillingness to debate an accomplished prosecutor who was armed with facts regarding her culpable behavior as well as her abuse of her prosecutorial powers and duties. There were just too many unanswered questions. It simply was not her intention to ever be held accountable for her conduct. She was Jeanine Pirro, after all, and there would be one standard of scrutiny for her, and a different one for everyone else.

In the days following the WTC attack that quickly became weeks, there was no room in either the broadcast or print news media for anything but related news items. That fact, in addition to the obvious bias of *The Journal News*, played very nicely into Jeanine's "stonewalling strategy." It wasn't as though she made no public appearances, however. She was very happy to leave her bunker to travel into New York City, accompanied by a photographer from *The Journal News* specifically to be seated in St. Patrick's Cathedral, close enough to Ed Koch so that she could be photographed grasping his hand. As he leaned forward, nearly falling from his pew, those around him looked on in disbelief.

Most politically astute observers have come to recognize that Ed Koch can not be taken too seriously at this stage of his career, and, given the enormous amount of scandal that permeated his administration, it is understandable that he could be cozy with the likes of Jeanine Pirro, and even kiss up to her for the cameras in a holy place in a sacred moment. One wonders if he had known of her ethnic rabble-rousing less than fifty days earlier whether he would still have "kosherized" her.

The Koch photo, which covered a half-page in *The Journal News,* was but one of Jeanine's many despicable exploitations of our national grief in the days immediately following the attack. She would be seen repeatedly in the company of Governor Pataki, often nudging her way in front of the cameras at numerous official ceremonies at which she really had no jurisdictional justification to be present.

Back home in Westchester she employed other political antics to exploit misery. Amongst those lost at the World Trade Center was Michael McHugh who had been the Republican candidate for a seat in the County Legislature held by Vito Pinto. His wife, Maria, a political novice, was granted judicial permission to

Photos by Seth Harrison/The Journal News

Westchester County District Attorney Jeanine Pirro, right, greets former New York City Mayor Ed Koch and U.S. Sen. Joseph Lieberman before the service.

run in his place. Jeanine Pirro could not pass up an opportunity to call a press conference to be seen with and to exploit the tragedy of Mrs. McHugh on the front steps of the Westchester County Office Building. Her need to gain some political advantage, even from the tragic circumstances of Mrs. McHugh and her family, was more than she and her advisors could resist.

We learned of her scheme less than half an hour before the scheduled appearance and we determined that it was necessary for Tony to be present and for him to make a public statement condemning such insensitive and immoral exploitation of such a victim. The whole episode came off very badly for Jeanine and essentially underscored her ruthless willingness to do whatever she deems necessary to promote herself politically no matter at whose expense.

Continuing to see the Trade Center tragedy as an ongoing political opportunity for her, Jeanine proceeded to upstage and offend her fellow Cabal members, Andy Spano and Larry Schwartz. Catching them by surprise, she publicly announced the establishment of a program within her office to comfort and counsel the families of the WTC victims. She knew full well, of course, that such support activity was clearly the purview and responsibility of the County Executive. But once again, she could not resist the opportunity to steal the political advantage of an announcement so pregnant with public sympathy and support.

Andy Spano and his point man, Larry Schwartz were unmistakably "pissed" with Jeanine for stealing the spotlight. *Is there no honor amongst thieves?* Or, was it simply a matter of every player for himself/herself? If it was the latter, no one could compete with Jeanine, the Prosecutor.

Consider the fact that while Jeanine succeeded in getting

Andy Spano to fire two of his most competent high-level deputies, Jay Hashmall and Robi Schlaff, she managed to hire two of her husband's supporters, one as an $87,000 Assistant District Attorney, and the other as a $34,000 Legal Secretary. A third Al Pirro stooge was steered to a $30,000 Law Clerk position in County Attorney Charlene Indelicato's office, having worked in the same capacity for six years for Al.

It says something about the relationship of The Cabal and the scope of the power and influence of Al Pirro that the individual whom she appointed to the ADA's position is Kevin Hynes, son of the DA of Brooklyn, Charles Hynes. At the time of Al's conviction, Kevin wrote to Judge Barrington Parker asking him not to send Al to prison. In his letter, dated August 15, 2000, he told the judge, "Al is a man of great generosity who took me under his wing and worked tirelessly to make my wife and me feel welcome." Hynes had just moved to Westchester County to set up a law firm in 1997. Apparently, even with all of the "fix it" man's help, he didn't fare too well in private practice.

Kevin Hynes' letter was just one of 120 letters received by Judge Parker, extolling Al's "generosity and kindness." Bill O'Shaughnessy, owner of WVOX radio station in New Rochelle went so far as to name Al Pirro "Man of the Year." Mayor Spencer of Yonkers, Putnam County DA Kevin Wright, and so many others who could not rightly be considered a part of the Jeanine Machine, wrote letters.

What on earth were these people thinking about? No matter what previous misimpression anyone may have held about Al Pirro, surely it should not have survived the ugly truth about his avoidance of child support payments for sixteen years, his attempts to blame his misconduct on his pathetic brother Anthony, or a score of other details that surfaced daily at the trial. What does it say about the morality of such petitioners that they would persist, even knowing if only for the first time, what kind of a guy Al really was?

Was he some kind of folk hero for screwing the IRS out of his fair share of taxes – at least on the legitimate income he bothered to report? Wasn't it enough that there was so much "under the table" that the "fix it" man would never report? What a stand up guy! What a "Man of the Year!"

Getting Rolling Again . . . Slowly

On Tuesday, September 25, exactly two weeks after all campaign activity ceased, we took our cue from President Bush to "get back to normal," whatever the new normal was to be. Once again, the three of us were back working the railroad. It was 6:30 AM at the Mt. Vernon West Railroad station and Hon. Richard Weingarten, a former Democratic Committee Chairman who was happy to help out greeting the morning commuters, joined us.

It felt good to be back in the saddle, if somewhat subdued by our nation's and our community's tragedy. People were once again very encouraging, if a little preoccupied. With less than six weeks to Election Day, we were forced to narrow our schedule somewhat to about forty stations, some days covering more than one.

The WCLA had twice postponed their planned news conference to announce their endorsement for D.A., out of deference to the events of September 11th, as well as their desire to have their just attention in the press. The freeze out continued at *The Journal News* even following my very frank exchange with their managing editor, CynDee Royale. I wondered just what kind of coverage the WCLA endorsement would receive in light of the fact that it had been front page news in prior campaigns when Jeanine had received it.

We didn't have any serious notion that Gary Sherlock's paper was about to be anything other than Mrs. Pirro's propaganda arm, and they did not disappoint us. The WCLA issued a press release clearly spelling out why they chose to endorse Tony and showing Jeanine for the impudent and vengeful person she was. *The Journal News,* coordinating with Pirro and the New York City Office of the National Abortion Rights Action League (NARAL), of no consequence in Westchester, printed an article headlined "Abortion Rights Groups Split On Pirro".

What a spin! What a manipulation of the facts.[20] Suddenly, the WCLA endorsement, which in years past was considered the single most important endorsement in Westchester, was relegated to the level of a New York City office of NARAL.

NARAL had sent out a five-question survey which Castro and Pirro had answered identically, a 'no-brainer' questionnaire. "So, why did you see fit to give your endorsement to Mrs. Pirro without so much as interviewing Mr. Castro?" I asked their attorney. The response was "whenever each candidate answers all five questions correctly, we give our endorsement to the incumbent." In reality, the NARAL endorsement was worthless, a rubber stamp available to the highest bidder.

The first of several parades was the Mt. Vernon Day Parade, which would prove most memorable for the pre-parade activity. It was September 29th, just a couple of days following Jeanine's public announcement that she was "suspending all campaign activity <u>indefinitely</u>" because someone she knew had supposedly been lost at the WTC. The staging area and starting point of the parade was in the north end of the city in a community known as Fleetwood.

As the first of six parades that candidates would march in for the six remaining weeks until the election, we had not put enough thought into volunteer distributors of palmcards or the carrying of signs. Tony was a little late in arriving and Jane M. and I stood amongst the politicians, candidates and marchers who were arriving and chatting. As we would be the only Castro people, we quickly decided that we would each cover one side of the line of march and proceed to distribute our palm cards to every possible spectator along the mile and a half route into the downtown business district.

Jeanine Pirro arrived shortly after we did. She was joined several minutes later by four or five of her workers including her campaign director and spokesperson, Ms. Mahoney, and her county-paid PR person, Ms. Corbalis. As Jeanine stood alone, Andy Spano, who was across the street, came running over and gave her the kind of hug and kiss that left **no doubt** in anyone's mind whose side **he** was on.

Jane M., a newcomer to politically working parades and to the false smiles and civility so often a part of such events was becoming agitated with Jeanine's presence in light of her public proclamation of abstinence just days before. I attempted to calm her, explaining that such statements and contradictions were all a part of the game for someone like Jeanine. But she remained upset and indignant that Jeanine would have lied to the public.

Finally, the sight of Corbalis and Mahoney arriving with a couple of volunteers all carrying Pirro signs was more than Jane could handle. As Jeanine came across the street in their company, Jane met them at the curb. I stood perhaps ten feet from Jane as she turned to Jeanine and said, "I thought you said you were suspending all campaign activity indefinitely!"

With fire in her eyes, Jeanine glowered, retorting, "WHO ARE YOU?"

Before the words came through Jeanine's teeth I was at Jane's side, arm on her shoulder, and I quipped, "It all depends on Mrs. Pirro's definition of *indefinitely*." With that remark, Corbalis, who was moving toward Jane, chilled, and further ugliness was avoided. For a few minutes, Jane, who never had any particular fondness for me, clung close as if having just been rescued by her big brother.

Jeanine had shown her real self. How dare an ordinary citizen question her conduct. "Who are you" meant "Who the fuck are you?!? How dare you! I don't have to answer to anyone, God damn it! I am Jeanine Pirro!"

She might be elected to public office and sworn to be a public servant in the eyes of the community, but in her eyes, she is a celebrity. As Steve Dunleavy, columnist for *The New York Post* once explained of dysfunctional celebrities, she thinks, "somehow, celebrity adulation, riches and privilege immunize (her) from basic regard for us common folk." Clearly, she is right. A person of her character, her sociopathic, ego-centered personality, surely can not be a public servant. Hers is clearly the persona of a celebrity, an actress . . . a very convincing actress, indeed, as Tony and I would come to discover.

On the evening of September 25, Tony was scheduled to attend an interview session with the Hispanic Police Officer's Association of Westchester for the purpose of seeking their endorsement. This would probably be the last such interview by a police agency. He was requested to arrive at 6:00 PM but knowing from several previous interviews that candidates are generally seen on a first-come basis, we decided to arrive at 5:30 PM.

We arrived as planned and sure enough, there was a sign-in sheet that Tony signed first. Candidates would be called in for interviews in the order in which they signed in. A few minutes after we arrived, Jeanine showed up with Ms. Mahoney.

Jeanine who is always dressed to kill, if outrageous for a DA, was wearing flats, an old, plain white blouse, a long and ill-fitting skirt and her hair was flat. She looked as though she had come to clean the office.

Although the four of us exchanged hellos, Jeanine and Mahoney remained in the hallway outside of the waiting room. They appeared to be rehearsing or prepping. Jeanine was actually "getting into character." To our credit, both Tony and I noticed how different she looked and acted. But 'acting' was exactly what she was up to, and neither of us realized just how cunning and calculated her appearance before the Hispanic Officers was going to be.

As she approached the sign-in sheet upon arrival, she made note of the fact that Tony had already signed in, to which Tony cracked a friendly remark joking, "Looks like you came in second." Little did we realize the joke was on us.

The understanding was that the endorsements would be announced at the organization's dinner dance. Tony had been interviewed by police departments and PBA's for months, always with the same result. They would say, typically, "Tony, we're impressed with you. But you know how it is. It's politics and we're forced to endorse her. But we're all voting for you." And that wasn't just the feeling of the rank and file.

I had invited the police commissioner of a large city in Westchester whom I had known for almost 20 years to have lunch with Tony just to get them acquainted because I felt pretty confident a month out that Tony could be the next DA. His response was, "I will have lunch with Tony the day after election however it comes out. I'm voting for Tony, and everyone in my family is. But if Jeanine finds out that I had lunch with him . . ."

We had reason to believe that the Hispanic officers might be different. Tony had pointed out to them that of the 118 attorneys in Jeanine's office; not one was a Latino. They needed no reminder of the fact that the only case she had ever decided she would prosecute as a capital case, Murder One, involved a Latino defendant.[21] Tony's fine reputation in the Bronx, and amongst other police agencies was well-known as compared with Mrs. Pirro who had boasted in the press that she had prosecuted 55 police and correction officers over eight years as District Attorney.

Attendance at the dinner dance was not inexpensive. It was $125 per person. Jeanine had purchased a whole table, 10 seats, and brought a contingent of Assistant DA's. Tony strolled over to their table early in the evening as he began to make the rounds and said, "I come not as a conqueror, but as a liberator." He was in a good mood, and the good-natured remark was as truthful as it was humorous.

But Jeanine was destined to have the last laugh. Venus Taylor, a policewoman from Yonkers who had been our contact person with the organization came to our table and took me aside. With disgust and frustration etched in her expression, she broke the news that the Hispanic Officers were going to endorse Jeanine. She and others who were in the minority were very upset.

I was upset and feeling a bit betrayed, sold out. "Why would they do that?" I asked. She said that when Jeanine was interviewed, the male officers thought she looked tired and overworked. They thought she was a hard working prosecutor and a single mom with Al away. As for Tony, he was "too sure of himself."

She had given an Academy Award performance and the *machismos* had fallen for it, hook, line, and sinker. Funny, how she didn't fool the women.

There will always be those who could be taken in by Jeanine. But, then there are those, who, despite realizing the evil, the criminality, the oppression, choose to collaborate. They are the most cowardly, much like the French who collaborated with their Nazi German occupiers. They must live with their consciences.

Such an individual is David Cohen, Dean of Pace University School of Law. His need to kiss-up to Jeanine Pirro, in spite of her outrageous misconduct and unbridled assault upon Freedom of Speech, falls nothing short of collaboration with the Enemy of Justice.

In June of 2000 as Al Pirro stood trial in Federal District Court in White Plains, Pace University Law Professor Bennett Gershman attended the trial, and was called upon by the press and media for commentary. Gershman who had been critical of Jeanine's antics for some time, was especially appropriate and qualified for the task. In the same emotional and unprofessional mode of conduct that she employed against Mary Jo White, Jeanine now threatened Dean Cohen that if he did not muzzle Gershman, she would never hire another Pace Law graduate.

Naturally, Cohen could not satisfy her demand had he wanted to. But, he would find a way to "kiss her ring." He invited Jeanine to be the Guest of Honor at the school's Awards Ceremony on October 4, 2001, just one month before Election Day.

I became aware of the situation many weeks before the scheduled event. It occurred to me that perhaps David Cohen, who had come to the Law School from Canada, might not be as aware of just how complicit Jeanine was in the criminal activities of her husband, or how willing she was to prosecute innocent individuals, such as my former client, merely to notch another conviction.

To his credit the Dean allowed me to make my case for more than an hour, but he would not be budged. I discovered how political and weak he was. He was determined to kiss-up to someone who had demanded that he muzzle Free Speech. I thanked the Dean and promised to memorialize his decision. His terse, yet patronizing, follow-up letter is shown below:

25th Anniversary
PACE LAW SCHOOL

DAVID COHEN
DEAN AND PROFESSOR OF LAW

78 NORTH BROADWAY
WHITE PLAINS, NY 10603
TELEPHONE (914) 422-4407
FACSIMILE (914) 422-4426
DCOHEN@LAW.PACE.EDU
HTTP://WWW.LAW.PACE.EDU

August 7, 2001

Richard Blassberg

Dear Richard:

I wanted to thank you for coming to see me. Your obvious commitment to our law school is something that I can only admire and wish for in all our alumni. I am sorry that my invitation to District Attorney Pirro concerns you, and as I explained, I believe that the law school ought to have the very best and strongest relationship with that office.

I am proud that you are one of our alumni.

Yours truly,

David Cohen
Dean of Law

The Yonkers Parade, October 7th, held in the southwest, predominantly Latino, corner of the City was in honor of Columbus Day. I was determined to bring a stronger contingent of Castro Volunteers than we had previously delivered. We came with seven women, including my twenty-year-old daughter, all wearing Castro T-shirts, carrying signs, and distributing palmcards.

Jeanine showed up with her paid cadre of "storm troopers" who went through the crowd giving out plastic Pirro garbage bags, and slapping self-sticking Pirro badges on everyone. Her campaign workers were as oppressive and offensive as Jeanine herself. Apparently, their idea was to create the illusion that there were great numbers of Pirro supporters. Their nastiness and forcefulness turned off many onlookers.

My daughter Deborah, who was in shoe sales with a major department store, had never seen Jeanine in person before. As the parade was lining up, and I pointed her out, Deborah turned to me and said, "She's wearing Stilettos. I'm surprised she wears Stilettos." Stilettos or not, Andy Spano was determined to march and stand right by Jeanine's side at each and every parade, right up to Election Day.

Tony had a very different approach to parades. He would work the crowds on each side of the street pressing the flesh and introducing himself to everyone he could possibly greet. He was a great hit with his boyish smile and his disarmingly sincere manner. He came off as a true "man of the people."

I would generally work the crowds together with our volunteers, well ahead of Tony, distributing his palmcard and asking thought provoking questions about Jeanine. I preferred, whenever possible, to follow her "storm troopers," so that I might make a remark such as, "I see you've gotten Mrs. Pirro's garbage bag. Now let me offer you a real district attorney," as I handed them a palmcard.

If he were close behind, I would point him out. Otherwise, I would simply say, "Tony will be along shortly to meet you and to discuss your concerns about the DAs Office."

Long after Jeanine and the other candidates had 'strutted on by,' Tony would still be working his way through the crowd. He genuinely enjoyed meeting the people, and was always especially pleased when individuals whom he had met before would come up to greet him. As Election Day drew closer he was rapidly becoming well known, despite *The Journal News*, and the distractions caused by the World Trade Center tragedy.

The Debate Debate.

From the very beginning of the campaign it was apparent that Jeanine Pirro's strategy would never allow for a public debate with Tony Castro. Of course, she had debated three times with Mike Chakasky in 1993, and five times with Joanne Naughton in 1997. That was then and this was now. She knew that she had too much baggage to risk a public debate with a skilled prosecutor such as Tony Castro. She also knew that despite her deal with Andy Spano, Castro was not a subscriber to the deal.

Jeanine's aversion to a debate scenario was further reinforced by her knowledge, as the weeks passed, that Ben and Jonathan, Carl, George, and I, were busy at work researching and investigating, and coming up with information from many sources. We knew that she knew because word got back to us that her "henchmen" had been tipped off and were following our visits to Federal Court, the public library, the County Clerk's Office, the Bureau of Land Records, and elsewhere.

Avoiding a debate, however became a more and more arduous task for Jeanine. Some invitations would be more difficult to turn down than others. The League of Women Voters proved to be a particularly difficult organization for her to sidestep. Unlike the Cable Television News Channel, one of the League's principal functions is to introduce various candidates for public office to voters through candidates nights and public debates. Debates are so very central to the League's mission that over the years they have developed several different formats.

In August, the New Rochelle League, in co-sponsorship with the New Rochelle Bar Association extended an invitation to Jeanine Pirro and Tony Castro to participate in a public debate on October 24th. We, of course, immediately accepted, and we were pleased to learn that Pirro had as well. On September 9th, Tony received a confirmation letter clearly indicating that "Mrs. Pirro had agreed to the debate." We were cautiously optimistic.

Our caution was justified. Within a few days following the World Trade Center attack, we received word from Gayle Golomb, President of the New Rochelle Chapter, that Jeanine was backing out of the debate. When we pressed for a reason we were told that her spokesperson, Sarah Gaffney Mahoney, had claimed that they never agreed to the event.[22]

Tony was not willing to be so lightly brushed aside, nor forced to accept Jeanine's unilateral control. We pressed Golomb for a legitimate reason, in light of the letter of confirmation we had received. Our insistence placed Golomb in an uncomfortable position since she could not deny that the League had also understood an acceptance by Jeanine. Golomb, as so many before her, was discovering that her credibility and integrity were in question for having allowed herself to be manipulated by the Jeanine Machine.

Faced with her own credibility gap, and under pressure not

to call the League liars, Jeanine once again used the World Trade Center tragedy, changing her story through her spokesperson to say she would not be able to attend the debate because of "conflicts in her schedule caused by the attack on the World Trade Center."[23] Of course, the debate was not scheduled to occur for more than five weeks.

We persisted, questioning why an alternate date could not be arranged; of course, knowing all along that no date would be acceptable to Jeanine. At one point, Gayle Golomb left me a phone message. "I am still negotiating with Mrs. Pirro's people, and will get back to you within four hours." Four hours became four days, and then four weeks. As October rolled on and we kept up the pressure for a debate, Jeanine found still, another excuse. She convinced Golomb to call off any possible debate because of "anticipated violations of their Fair-Campaign Pledge by Castro."[24] Tony might ask questions Jeanine did not want to answer about her own culpable conduct.

Eventually, the issue became very public, despite *The Journal News*. Cable News Channel 12 became involved because they too had been trying to set up a televised debate with Pirro. With time growing short, the County League of Women Voters Executive Board took the New Rochelle League to task, criticizing Golomb and others, and setting up their own Candidates' Debate in White Plains.

What had upset the County League was what columnist Phil Reisman described in his October 23rd column in *The Journal News*, as a "misguided (if not suspiciously conspiratorial) decision by the New Rochelle Chapter of the League of Women Voters to cancel a forum between the candidates, because of Tony Castro's alleged violation of a Fair-Campaign Pledge." Simply stated, the

County League did not want to appear to be taking sides with Jeanine Pirro by determining in advance what constituted a legitimate issue for debate - specifically Jeanine's own involvement in the culpable conduct of her husband.

It is important to note that Phil Reisman, as a columnist, enjoys a great deal of latitude in his selection of subject matter and expression of opinion. Unlike news reporters, only his accounts, throughout the campaign, were free from censorship or revision by management. That fact was in their own best interest, given the quality and popularity of Phil's column.

On October 20th *The Journal News* published an article quoting Jeanine Pirro declaring that she would not debate Tony Castro at all because she objected to his alleged "underhanded tactics and negative personal attacks."[25] This was her final excuse for not facing her opponent, or the people of Westchester, in public debate. She was simply not willing to face public scrutiny, or to be held accountable for the kinds of conduct no district attorney should have ever engaged in.

The First Annual White Plains Hispanic Day Parade was scheduled for kick-off at twelve noon. Given her press release, I was not about to let her off easy. I decided, for this parade, to change my tactics. I would not follow her storm-troopers. This time I would get rolling ahead of them, carrying as many palmcards as possible, and carrying one important message.

I would approach clusters of folks lined up awaiting the parade. Holding up a palmcard with Tony's picture, I would ask, "Does this man look like The Big Bad Wolf?" After the laughter, I would follow with, "Then why is Mrs. Pirro afraid to debate him?"

Sometimes I went further, "Honestly folks, Tony is a prosecutor. Only criminals are afraid of prosecutors." I could tell my remarks were resonating with the crowd. Jeanine was becoming a laughing-stock.

About two blocks into my mission, I noticed Mahoney and Corbalis moving toward my position on the opposite side of the street. Allowing them to catch up at a point where the crowd was heavy, I called out to them, "What's the matter, cat got Mrs. Pirro's tongue?" They were silent. I came back with, "Has she got laryngitis?" "Poor Jeanine, she's lost her voice and can't debate Tony Castro!"

I was trying to 'get their goat' and apparently succeeded. Jeanine couldn't make it half way through the parade before she grabbed a microphone from a News Channel 12 reporter. With the veins in her neck popping, she screamed into the camera, "I'll debate Mr. Castro, anytime, anywhere!" Her news release hadn't been on the street quite six hours, and she was already reversing herself. I had rained on her parade.

Despite her ugly, emotional outburst, everyone knew she would never face Tony in debate. In the two weeks to election Tony would appear at the County League of Women Voters, to debate an empty chair, and make a similar appearance on News Channel 12, "Newsmakers" Program, which aired all weekend prior to election. Naturally, *The Journal News* covered neither forum.

<u>The New York Times, The Journal News</u>

Every candidate for public office would like to receive as many endorsements as possible. Certain types of endorsements such as from unions, or police benevolent associations may be beneficial if members are inclined to perceive some direct benefit in electing one candidate over another. Usually, that kind of job-related candidate preference is associated with legislative or executive office – a mayor, a county legislator, or a county executive.

Most intelligent voters realize, however, that union and benevolent association endorsements are political trade-offs of one kind or another and are less likely to be influenced if they are not organization members. Newspaper endorsements are supposed to be of a different stripe. While most major daily newspapers have long ago established their perch on the continuum of liberalism and conservatism, and can usually be depended upon to support candidates and view issues in ways consistent with their site, still a newspaper endorsement can be worth so much more.

For one thing, unless one is dealing with a situation such as the marriage of *The Journal News* with Jeanine Pirro, the outcome of endorsement interviews by newspaper editors is often in doubt. Newspapers, when honestly operated, have an obligation to their readers and indeed to the community they purport to serve to be objective, fair and unbiased in their evaluations and recommendations. Are they always?

In 2001, Gary Sherlock, publisher and president of *The Journal News,* spent hundreds of thousands of dollars on radio and television airtime pursuing an ad campaign whose central theme was that his newspaper was "the way you know." Taking the microphone in hand, Sherlock professed a "fair and balanced presentation of the news," reminding all who might listen that a free press was at the heart of our democratic institutions from the very beginning of our nation. Of course, those of us who witnessed the shameless bias and blatant spinning of news to favor Mrs. Pirro, a practice that continued to this writing, know full well why *The Journal News* spends a fortune trying to convince the community that they are "on the level."

<u>Recent Case in Point:</u>

On March 4, 2002, attorney Randolph Scott-McLaughlin called a press conference in White Plains (the home city of *The Journal News*) to announce a 20 million dollar law suit against Jeanine Pirro and the County of Westchester. Attorney Scott-McLauglin, a Professor at Pace University Law School, also in White Plains, charged Mrs. Pirro with causing severe physical and psychological harm to his client as a result of her mishandling of information and refusal to provide customary protections generally afforded to stalking victims.

In the evening of March 4, every major network and regional television station featured the story on their evening and nightly news editions. On Tuesday, March 5, *The New York Times* ran it in their Metro Section, including a photo of Jeanine. *The Journal News* was absolutely silent on the matter; nothing, nada!

On Thursday, October 25, 2001, Tony and I took Metro North from White Plains into Manhattan. Our destination was William Street in Lower Manhattan, the offices of George Artz, our press and publicity agents. We were meeting our associate, Bob Liff, who had been editing and reformatting our press releases and arranging and attending some of our press conferences.

Neither Tony nor I had been in lower Manhattan in the six weeks following the Trade Center collapse. Walking through the normally narrow streets, now further narrowed by hastily constructed wooden channels carrying electric and phone cables and other services lining each side of the roadway at the curb, one had the sense of a return to another time. There was a distinct lack of sound and activity normally encountered there. It was altogether eerie.

There was no time for reflection. We were on a mission. We had come down essentially to prepare Tony for his *New York Times* endorsement interview. Tony was scheduled to be seen the following day by Dorothy Samuels, editorial board member, a contact that George Artz had made. Earlier in the morning, Tony had interviewed for endorsement at *The Journal News* with Jeanine, and he joked as we traveled into the City, "After the session this morning, I really don't need any prepping for *The Times.*"

We were met in the lobby at 10 William Street by Bob for security reasons, and brought to a conference room where George Artz and another associate briefed and instructed Tony, and generally chatted about things for a half hour over coffee and pastries. Somebody, perhaps Bob, got the bright idea that since we had come all the way down from White Plains, perhaps Ms. Samuels, if she were available, would see Tony and save us a second trip.

Tony, Bob and I emerged from the subway at Broadway and 42nd Street, Times Square.. Things were clearly quieter, more subdued than usual. Security at the Times Building was very tight. We were joined by an assistant from the editorial department, who escorted us to Ms. Samuels' office. As we left the elevator, something George Artz had said as we were leaving our earlier meeting came back to me. He had told Tony, "If she spends half an hour with you, you have a chance. If she gives you 45 minutes, that's a good sign."

Samuels occupied a rather small office given her power and position with *The Times*. A woman in perhaps her early to mid-fifties, she had no airs or pretence about her. She was remarkably familiar with events and people in the Westchester and metropolitan New York area, even given her occupation. She was very curious about our effort and quite knowledgable about Jeanine. Of course, she did not know Jeanine in the same detail as we did, but she was clearly not at all taken in by her.

Apparently, Ms. Samuels had been getting a "run-a-round" from both Jeanine and her mouthpiece, Mahoney, regarding Jeanine's availability for an endorsement interview. At one point, Samuels indicated that she had been lied to by the Pirro camp. I took that to mean that Tony might have a good chance of winning the prize.

Naturally, Tony did most of the talking, but at one point I felt it would be appropriate to share the story of my former client's eight-month long ordeal at Jeanine's hands. She was very interested and thoroughly engrossed in the saga.

At one point, she called in another member of the editorial board to sit in on the session. She took notes throughout the meeting and asked for specifics that suggested she was intending to check out our credibility. No one was paying any particular attention to the time as we talked about one subject after another.

Finally, when almost ninety minutes had passed, I looked at my watch and broke in to remind Tony that we had a train to catch if we were going to make it to a 6:00 PM fundraiser in Tarrytown. We apologized for having to leave, and thanked her for her time and consideration. As we hit the street, walking quickly towards Grand Central, I gleefully reminded Tony of what George Artz had said, "Tony, we were there about 90 minutes and she would have kept you longer. That's got to be a good sign."

We had left behind with Dorothy Samuels a book of approximately 150 pages that we referred to as our "white paper on Jeanine Pirro." It contained material from the transcript of the tax fraud trial, from the federal indictment and from newspaper accounts that raised very serious questions in seven specific areas of culpable behavior by Jeanine Pirro. We had come prepared to back up our statements concerning her lack of fitness to hold the office of District Attorney.

Of course, very serious questions concerning Mrs. Pirro had been raised more than a year earlier in a *New York Times* editorial on June 22, 2000, two days after her husband's conviction on all counts in US District Court. To date, Jeanine has never come clean, has never explained her hands-on culpable involvement as a co-conspirator in the tax fraud, nor her failure to prevent, prosecute or expose criminal activities from which she personally benefited.

The endorsement interview at *The Journal News* was a totally different scenario from the one at the *New York Times*, or any of the weekly publications Tony had visited. *The Journal News* had no fewer than twelve staff; two from their editorial board, Milton Hoffman and Ron Patafio; nine reporters and a columnist, and their president/publisher Gary Sherlock, who dropped by just to keep an eye on things.

Both candidates were present. Jeanine arrived with Ms. Mahoney and two male assistants, each carrying a large cardboard box filled with files. Tony and I came to the process knowing full well, based on months of biased coverage, that he didn't stand a 'snowball's chance in hell' of getting their endorsement. Several of the reporters present would later reveal their disgust over their employer's sham ceremony and predetermined endorsement. We were not disappointed.

The Journal News endorsement came out on Tuesday, October 30 – exactly one week before Election Day. It touted the same lines we had heard from Ms. Mahoney right along. It was long on praise for Jeanine and very short on facts. It even went so far as to reassert her lie that she had founded the Domestic Violence Unit, a falsity for which Carl Vergari had rebuked Jeanine in their very newspaper just four years earlier.[26] It was everything we expected would come from a newspaper with no local competition that was, in fact, a propaganda arm of the *Jeanine Machine*.

It's important to know that at *The Journal News* session, Tony slid the "white paper" across the table to the editorial board members, Patafio and Hoffman, in response to Jeanine's comment that, "Mr. Castro's allegations are all baseless." Not only did they totally disregard its contents in making their "decision" to endorse Jeanine, but they also saw to it that it disappeared, never to be seen by any of their reporters.[27]

The last ten days before election were very hectic as we continued to greet commuters from 6:30 to 8:30 each morning, attended senior citizen housing and recreational centers in the afternoons, and civic and religious centers at night. Weekends were filled with parades, picnics and fundraisers. The schedule was more crowded than originally anticipated as organizations began to spring back to life several weeks after the attack. Everywhere he went, Tony Castro was a big hit. He was especially popular with senior citizens who seemed most able to see through Jeanine's mythological image.

A group of about forty concerned Republicans, many of them friends of Richard DiGuglielmo, ran a fundraiser for Tony. A New York City transit police officer, whom Jeanine had tried for second degree murder, DiGuglielmo had shot and killed a man who was attacking his elderly father with a metal baseball bat. The case had been a Jeanine Pirro classic, with extensive pre-trial press releases and posturing in the media to make it appear that the incident was a racially motivated bias crime. The facts of the case clearly indicated otherwise. The deceased, a black sanitation worker from White Plains with a record of ten arrests and a propensity for violence, had become physically assaultive with the defendant's father who had placed a "no-parking" sticker on the window of his late model Corvette. The car had been parked in a "Customers Only" parking lot of the elder DiGuglielmo's deli in Dobbs Ferry while the deceased went across the street for pizza.

After the defendant intervened with the assistance of his brother-in-law, the deceased was wrestled to the ground and released unharmed. At this point, still upset about the sticker on his Corvette, the deceased grabbed a metal bat from his trunk and began once more assaulting the defendant's father. This time, the defendant ran into his father's deli, grabbed his father's revolver, and shot and killed the attacker.

It was clearly a tragic and unnecessary loss of life, but it was not a bias crime. There was no reason to believe the outcome would have been any different had the attacker been white. Richard DiGuglielmo, a police officer trained to shoot to kill, was using deadly force to prevent the use of deadly force by the deceased against his father.[28]

Many who were close to the case and attended the trial were convinced that Jeanine withheld exculpatory information while spinning the facts of the case into a crime of racial hatred and unjustifiable homicide. Overcharged and tried first in the press, Richard DiGuglielmo was convicted and sentenced to twenty years. His friends and family had a very special reason to support Tony Castro.

As the moment of truth was but a few days away, we wondered when and if *The New York Times* was going to announce its endorsement. We believed that based on the objective facts, Tony deserved their support. We were realistic enough to recognize that it would take considerable courage and honesty for those who would make the decision to overcome not only Jeanine's media image but also her pull with heavyweights in the media.

Many supporters, including volunteers close to Tony, were very doubtful about the endorsement. I found myself feeling somewhat angered by such defeatist thinking and at the same time, needing to reassure the faithful that we were going to pull it off. I had been there with Tony and I just could not allow myself to believe *The New York Times* would kiss her ring, too. Finally, just ninty-six hours before the polls would open, Friday before Election Day, *The Times* endorsed Tony Castro for District Attorney of Westchester with the following:

For D.A. in Suffolk and Westchester

The noisiest election contests in Suffolk and Westchester Counties this fall are those for district attorney. Both races pit active Democratic challengers against veteran Republican incumbents. Here are our recommendations:

Suffolk County: After a dozen years in office, Suffolk's district attorney, the Republican James Catterson, can claim some real accomplishments, including innovative efforts to divert low-level dealers to treatment, crack down on drunken-driving offenders and protect battered woman. But his record is marred by bullying behavior and bad judgment calls, like his decision to continue to solicit contributions from his employees even as he was prosecuting a local sheriff for using his office to do political work.

Our endorsement goes to Democratic opponent, Thomas Spota. A defense attorney in private practice and a former assistant district attorney, he offers solid experience, along with fresh ideas for bolstering an office lately beset by an alarmingly high rate of staff turnover.

Westchester County: During eight years in office, District Attorney Jeanine Pirro has energetically tackled both lower-level crime and more serious felonies. She had made good use of special bureaus that focus on key areas like environmental crime, child abuse and domestic and gang violence. But while there is much to admire about Ms. Pirro's record, the lingering cloud created by her husband's federal tax-fraud conviction prevents us from supporting her re-election.

No one in this era of working couples wants to unfairly punish Ms. Pirro for bad behavior of her spouse. But she was not merely a victim of her husband's chicanery. She was a beneficiary who signed some of the tax returns that figured in his case. Her refusal to publicly discuss the particulars of her role in some of the tangled transactions that resulted in his now serving a 29-month prison sentence is troubling. Troubling, too, is her refusal to debate her Democratic challenger, Tony Castro, a Bronx district attorney's office.

Westchester residents deserve a district attorney untainted by swirling integrity and judgment questions. Ms. Pirro's mistakes cannot be dismissed as merely personal, as their inevitable consequence had been to share information.

Our endorsement goes to Mr. Castro. Although a newcomer to politics, he is a seasoned prosecutor whose election would give Westchester a vigorous crime-fighting district attorney with a record unblemished by scandal.

The endorsement was straightforward and Tony and those of us closest to him were relieved and grateful for it. The question was, having come at the last possible minute, would it be useful? With so little time left, we needed to distribute copies of it everywhere. We decided to use Kinkos to print 25,000 copies of it and quickly organized teams of volunteers to distribute it all over the County. It was important to have more than just a moral victory in the endorsement.

Tony got the endorsement, all right, and those readers who bothered to read the editorial page and wade through all of the races in the area would probably find it. However, in the Metro Section of the same edition, there was Jeanine's laughing face being declared a probable "easy winner" by *The Times* Westchester reporter, Randal Archibold. The timing was no coincidence. Jeanine had struck again.

That same morning, the *New York Law Journal* featured a front-page article and photo of Tony Castro. The reporter, Lori Tripoli, had taken the time and trouble to attend the County League of Women Voters Forum where Tony debated an empty chair a few days earlier. *The Law Journal* had run a puff feature on Jeanine several months earlier and really owed this last minute coverage to her opponent.

Tony worked right up to Election Day greeting commuters and visiting several senior housing complexes in Yonkers. He worked until he was physically drained. We were truly inspired and felt a deep obligation to so many who had given of themselves because they believed in Tony and had seen the light. On the eve of election, I felt that we had done everything possible, given September 11, that we could have done.

Yes, we regretted not having more time and not having raised

$100,000 more as a result of the terrorist attack. But we could only play the hand we were dealt, and make the best of it. As Tony was fond of saying, "the campaign was like a trial." We had presented the evidence and now the verdict was in the hands of the jury.

||| Eight |||

The Lessons of War

Once, nearly thirty years ago, I ran for Supervisor of the Town of Southeast, New York, sharing an independent ticket with a fellow I really didn't know well enough to have partnered up with. It turned out, as I discovered in the course of an eight-month campaign, that my running mate had built a swimming pool for the man I was running against, a five-time incumbent. The pool had collapsed! Also, my running mate had had other problems of personal conduct, which I would not have subscribed to.

When the campaign was over and I had come so very close to winning, much closer than my running mate, it became obvious to many that my association with this fellow had probably cost me the election. I was only 32 at the time, and a reporter who was even younger asked how come I had chosen to run with a man who had such liabilities? My response was, "Perhaps if there had been a longer engagement, there might not have been a marriage."

Running for public office, especially for the first time, as Tony Castro was, is often like that. One gets swept up in the spirit and the promise of the moment, the excitement necessary to overcome the inertia and the usual caution. If all first-time candidates really stopped to consider the time, money and effort they and their loved ones were about to expend, few would go forward. Given the name recognition, the funding and the election fixing activities of the Jeanine Machine, all of which were realized by him, Tony Castro was truly a candidate of unusual courage and confidence. He saw something that was wrong, very wrong, and wanted to make it right.

From the very outset, the race for District Attorney of Westchester was a classic face-off, and were it not for Jeanine Pirro's power to fix and extort, it would have had a story-book ending. Unlike so many contests these days, where voters are confronted with the choice between a "D-" and an "F" this was truly a "good vs. evil" scenario. And, evil was fighting for its life. There was no question that it was 'do, or die' for Jeanine.

For Castro, there would be obstacles that could have been anticipated and others that could never have been imagined. In the end, it would be the latter that would determine the outcome. In fact, there were three such crucial factors that Tony could not have taken into account before accepting the Democratic Party nomination on the evening of May 24, 2001. Had any one of the three not occurred, Jeanine would likely be a TV talk show host today.

The Journal News

The unanticipated role played by *The Journal News*, omitting, slanting, and reversing press releases, as well as putting a "Pirro spin" on all relevant news, clearly cost Castro the election. Their blatantly biased and shameless activity clearly qualified them as a first-class propaganda arm of Jeanine's campaign. Gary Sherlock and his rag were good for one thing – wrapping fish!

The Independence Party Endorsement

Jeanine's extortion of the Independence Party nomination represented the most clearly numerically quantifiable difference in the election results. The 7,821 votes cast on their line represented a "swing" of nearly sixteen thousand which would have made Tony Castro District Attorney by more than 3,000.

It is a testimonial to the fear and intimidation by which the Jeanine Machine survives that nearly five months after the election Dr. Cavallo would attempt to deny what he had said to Tony Castro, on May 24th 2001, and to Democratic Election Commissioner Reggie Lafayette , immediately after the election of November 6th. Despite the fact that Dennis Wedra was acquitted on all counts in the long delayed election fraud trial, Jeanine Pirro's threat to indict the good doctor not only bought his party's endorsement, but also his silence ever after.

In an editorial on the front page of *The Harrison Independent,* a weekly newspaper, editor Ralph Martinelli, in the February 21, 2002 edition, produced an account headlined, "How D.A. Pirro Stole the Independence Party Line." In it he reported that Dr. Guilio Cavallo and Mario Castaldo, the two leaders who "basically control who gets endorsed by their party" were set to endorse Tony Castro for District Attorney. However, according to Martinelli, "Pirro's campaign put on the full court press on the Independence Party Executive Committee." And, "phone calls were made to committee members at 2 AM" putting pressure on them to endorse Jeanine.

At the time of these public disclosures, neither Dr. Cavallo nor any of his committee members had seen fit to contact Tony Castro since the afternoon of May 24th when Cavallo had said "we want you and we will endorse you for DA, but, she scares and intimidates us."

Tony thought it was about time Cavallo spoke with him, and decided to invite him to lunch in New Rochelle. Upon receiving the phone call, Cavallo was apologetic, almost confessional, according to Tony, and he agreed to lunch a few days later. Surely, he had every reason to be apologetic, as he had remorsefully acknowledged to Commissioner Lafayette months earlier.

When Tony arrived he was surprised to discover that Cavallo had brought Dhyalma Vasquez, who had also been present when Cavallo had proclaimed his intentions and his fears back in May. To Castro's surprise, Cavallo struck a less than cordial tone, asking him, "Who put you up to this?" Although assured that Tony felt it was a good idea to meet and clarify what had happened, because he intended to remain active in Westchester affairs and might very likely run again, Cavallo remained defensive and argumentative. He denied ever having said that he and his party were afraid of Jeanine or intimidated by her. Going to ridiculous lengths, he declared, "Mrs. Pirro is afraid of me!"

Cavallo went on to tell Tony Castro that the reason Jeanine got the Independence Party endorsement was because the Republicans made him a better offer than the Democrats were willing to make. One can but wonder how fearful he must still be of Jeanine, to be willing to place himself and his party in the position of having told Tony they would endorse him because of what he stood for, and then renege because they were bought off with promises of patronage. The only promise he responded to was Jeanine Pirro's that she would indict and involve him in the election fraud trial the Wedra jury tossed out, if she did not get the endorsement. Nothing is more persuasive than hearing at 2AM "it's your bull that's about to get gored!"

The World Trade Center Attack

Obviously nobody could have imagined what occurred on September 11, 2001. The impact of that cowardly attack upon our way of life will likely be felt for generations to come. For Tony Castro's campaign it was a crippling event which stopped his forward movement just as momentum was building. For more than a month, fundraising was all but impossible. And the focus of the Nation, particularly New York, was solely on the results of the attack.

In financial terms, the Castro campaign lost more than $100,000 which could not be made up even when activity resumed. The loss of public interest and attention, especially in light of *The Journal News'* marriage to Jeanine, compounded the problem and probably was partly responsible for the lower-than-expected turn-out at the polls. Voters are strange sometimes. They will tell you after an election, "I would have come out to vote for you if I thought you would do so well." Consider Eliot Spitzer, Democratic State Attorney General of New York. (A position quite possibly next on Jeanine's list.) Spitzer called Castro the day after the election to offer his congratulations for his fine performance and to say, "If I thought you would do this well, I would have given you $50,000." Even well meant talk is cheap! All the "would've, should've and could've" only exacerbate the pain of knowing what good might have come from having fought the good fight.

It is as though, in the minds of some voters, casting their ballot is like betting on a horse race. They only want to vote for the winner. They seem to lose sight of the fact that by voting, unlike betting, they may directly determine the outcome of the event.

Perhaps it has something to do with the mentality of our younger generation that causes them to want to wear jerseys and sweats with the name of a celebrity sports figure. Maybe it's not cool to support anyone other than the sure winner. Maybe that was the message reporter Archibold was trying to spread for Jeanine in the Metro Section of *The Times*, the day Tony got their endorsement.

It's never easy to predict with any certainty what the voting public is likely to do - not just how they will vote, but whether they will come out at all. I thought that, if anything, the World Trade Center attack almost two months earlier, would have angered most Americans and strengthened their resolve to exercise their freedom of choice. Apparently, based upon the numbers, it did not.

We had calculated that a strong turnout would favor Tony Castro, because we reasoned that the election, from the start, was Jeanine's to lose. It was a certainty that she was not going to gain any new fans. She needed to try to retain as many misguided supporters as she could. Hers was a game plan of *damage control* – ours was one of *conversion.* We were winning the war, but time simply ran out[29].

It is widely recognized that incumbency offers a great advantage to nearly every candidate for public office. In fact, there are few situations in which being the incumbent would lessen one's chances. The incumbent generally has done favors, distributed funds and patronage, and possibly passed legislation favorable to large numbers of constituents, thus obligating support.

Over the years, as mounting political campaigns have become more and more media intensive and costly, the advantages of incumbency have become so influential that some federal, state, and municipal offices have been made subject to term-limits by statute. The need for term limits regarding the Presidency, for example, was recognized more than half a century ago as FDR was elected for a fourth term. Opponents back then complained that his administration was becoming a monarchy, and that was before television.

It is no secret that once an individual becomes comfortable and entrenched in his position he is often unwilling to give up the celebrity, the limelight and the perks he has enjoyed. Right in New York alone there are two outstanding examples. Rudy Giuliani,

Mayor of the City of New York for two terms – eight full years – tried for some time to find a way to circumvent the term limit he knew was in effect when he took office in 1994.

Governor George Pataki ran in 1994 on a promise that he would only serve for two terms, having defeated Mario Cuomo who was trying for his fourth. Pataki would like everyone to forget that promise, because he realizes he has nowhere else to go now.

As important as it is to recognize the need for term limits in the executive branches of Government, somehow our state and federal law makers have failed to recognize and deal with the problems inherent in the judiciary, most notably, state Attorneys General and District Attorneys. It is high time state legislators took notice of the unusually long tenure of prosecutors who are re-elected term after term virtually for life.

One may argue that if they are doing a good job and the voting public sees fit to reelect such DAs, what's the problem? The problem is not in the election; it's in the nomination! The problem is that only a prosecutor has the power to save or destroy lives, particularly under our system of justice where more than 95% of all criminal indictments are disposed of with a plea bargain. The problem is that the political power brokers who turn the wheels that spin out the candidates are often themselves vulnerable to, and fearful of, the power of a prosecutor to do harm to their constituents, or to them.

In short, prosecutors are feared often by the very people in the best position to perpetuate their control. In the case of Jeanine Pirro, Andy Spano, a man who could not lose, no matter who the Republicans might have run against him, betrayed his party, his running mates, and, most importantly, the people of Westchester County, in his disgraceful deal to re-elect Jeanine. How much dirt must she have on him? How pathetic and small of character, this person elected with a 72% plurality.

Of course, Jeanine is unique, even amongst those prosecutors who have wielded such influence over their own re-election. She is the spouse of a federal felon, whose criminal activity is legend within the same jurisdiction in which she purports to be the chief law enforcement officer. What's more, she herself is culpable with respect to many of his criminal activities, both as a co-conspirator and as a shield from prosecution. She is nothing short of a common criminal, and those most responsible for her return to power are fully aware of her sins.

Confronted with the facts as they are, one does not remove such a stubborn stain from the fabric of one's community by expecting the periodic election process to perform the purge. If any lesson has come from the campaign against Jeanine Pirro it is simply this: You can not succeed against an evil, so well entrenched, so well financed, by merely bringing out the truth, on crutches, every four years!

The effort must be on-going, toe to toe. Each and every opportunity to confront the lie with truth must not be missed. Sober arguments based on reason and logic must repeatedly challenge the spin, the myth, and the lies continually employed by an evil such as the Jeanine Machine.

Old ideas, much as old habits, do not die easily. Some individuals' minds will be forever made up, and those persons will not want to be *confused with facts.* Still others have held their mythological heroine in such esteem for so long that they will "not be able to handle the truth." Fortunately, most individuals are more open-minded and receptive.

As obvious as it may seem, it comes down to the three M's:

Money, Message and Management. Provided, of course, the candidate is credible and compatible with his message, wise management, especially as regards appropriate issues and exposure, coupled with enough money to reach the target population, comprise the fundamental formula.

Tony Castro was a most credible candidate, with 14 outstanding years in the Bronx DA's office, perhaps the toughest county in all of New York State to prosecute crime. He was completely compatible with his simple message: "The restoration of honesty and integrity to the Westchester D.A.'s Office." Try as they may, Jeanine's spinmasters could find no chink in his armor.

Unlike Jeanine Pirro, he did not come off as a one-dimensional image. People who met him were immediately impressed by his genuineness and his down-to-earth personality. They seemed to grasp quickly that he was for real.

Fortunately, even assuming Jeanine Pirro is still the District Attorney of Westchester in 2005, the effort to unseat her will have been enhanced by what has already been achieved. Having won by only six percentage points, and then only through extortion and political fraud, Jeanine's myth of invincibility has been pierced. Unable to accept that she is no longer "Westchester's Darling," her post-election media blitz, coupled with her abuse of prosecutorial powers against Jay Hashmall, Dennis Wedra, and others, has already begun to lay bare her evil and corrupt agenda.

Even before judicial action can be brought against her by individuals whose constitutional rights have been so trampled by her fury, she has set in motion a process that can only be self-destructive. She can not help herself. As with so many tyrants throughout history, she must continually convince herself that she is all-powerful and virtually answerable to no one.

Predictably, once she becomes the target of a civil action and/or a criminal investigation into her official and personal misconduct, the Jeanine Machine will unravel from the inside out. The Cabal, the rotten core, will melt down first, as those players, Andy Spano, Larry Schwartz, Nick Spano, and others most implicated in her fraud and corruption, seek to deny and disavow their culpability. It will only take one revealing court action to set off the chain reaction that will spin out of her control.

At this writing cracks have begun to appear. The Wedra acquittal was a very serious blow, not only to her ego and her agenda, but also to her long-standing modus operandi with politically important prosecutions and trials. Her relentless, vindictive, harassment of Jay Hashmall in pursuit of her thirst for blood and raw unchallenged power, has already begun to expose other members of the cabal to scrutiny. One can but imagine Andy Spano pleading, "Enough already, Jeanine!"

||| Nine |||

Beyond The Reign Of Terror

Reclaiming and Restoring the District Attorney's Office

When United States Attorney Mary Jo White elected not to include Jeanine in the tax fraud indictment she made a bad judgment call. First, she misjudged the morality and the sensibility of the people of Westchester, assuming Jeanine's so-called popularity would overcome the "mountain of evidence" upon which Al was convicted on all counts.

Second, she misjudged Jeanine. She obviously believed that upon Al's conviction, the information which would come out at trial, seriously implicating Jeanine, would be enough to end her occupation of the District Attorney's Office. Mary Jo did not understand the sociopathic nature of Jeanine's personality, nor the level of corruption that she and her cabal were capable of. She did not understand how her decision would help perpetuate Jeanine's administration, by making it appear as though "Jeanine wasn't guilty, only Al was." She contributed to the evil in the D.A.'s office by lacking the conviction to go after it.

Loss of the D.A.'s office would have been more devastating to Jeanine than to most. Without the power of the position, she would have been a crab without claws. She would have been vulnerable, and so would her "meal-ticket," Al.

Loss of the power to prosecute would have been painful for her in a more subtle way as well. She is essentially a non-conformist at heart, not that non-conformity is necessarily a bad thing. However, Jeanine's is of the "thumb your nose" variety, with no particularly redeeming social agenda. Examples are everywhere in her conduct and demeanor.

Stripped of her powers, she might easily be mistaken for just any inappropriately dressed woman walking into court in her four-inch stilettos, miniskirt, and black embroidered stockings. Stripped of her powers, she could no longer defy judicial gag orders. Stripped of her powers, she could not continue her "masquerade of innocence" or her refusal to acknowledge her own culpable conduct.

The District Attorney's Office Under Jeanine

The Westchester County District Attorney's Office is really the Jeanine Pirro District Attorney's Office. Some time ago Jeanine made certain that everybody understood that fact by doing something no prior D.A. had ever done. Without County authorization, or approval, she changed the official shield to read Jeanine Pirro, District Attorney, Westchester County.

In a perfect world, every prosecutor would be as concerned with protecting the innocent as prosecuting the guilty. They would follow-up serious claims of innocence to be certain they were not prosecuting innocent individuals. They would not obsess over obtaining the highest possible conviction rate, any conviction, so long as it's a conviction.

However, even in the real world, Jeanine's operation is extreme. It is all about herself. Her highest priority is self-promotion. Every decision, no matter how small the case, must come through her, and the overarching criterion is, "How might this promote my image?" Thus, the administration of justice is warped, and often unnecessarily slowed, in order to accommodate her purpose.

Her investigations do not ask the question, "What actually happened here?" Instead, she starts from the premise, "How can we arrive at a conviction of the accused?"

Jeanine's Internet sting operation fits her self-promotional agenda perfectly. It is what prosecutors call "lock and load," like catching fish in a tub. At this writing, she boasts 50 arrests with 44 convictions. She claims a 100% conviction rate. But, once again, with Jeanine, it's all about image versus reality.

Unlike a spontaneous criminal act, a "lock and load" defendant has been lured into a circumstance completely of the prosecutor's making and completely under her control. The witnesses are law enforcement personnel, paid and always willing to testify. The evidence is always ample, because the trap will not be sprung unless, and until, it is. Those cases which fail to achieve the necessary evidentiary threshold, are never heard about. So, why not a 100% conviction rate? She only prosecutes "100% airtight cases."

The real question is, "What are these so-called pedophiles convicted of?" Apparently, nothing too serious, given the fact that of the 44 who have been convicted, only 6 have done any jail-time, and most of those served for just a few days. Considering that such defendants were not, in fact, "chatting with a minor," but with an adult, at most they are guilty of "attempt."

What is troubling is the fact that of her first 50 arrests, only 15 had been found to have ever had any other inappropriate contact with a minor. Given that fact, and knowing that true pedophiles are repeat offenders, one must consider how many essentially innocent person's lives have been destroyed. How many have been wrecked on the theory that, "if they can be lured into attempting something they have never done, then they were surely predisposed, and would eventually have done it anyway?"

In other words, the operation is a prophylactic, a condom. Can we ever know whether the 70% of those who have been arrested, and will be arrested, who have committed no other inappropriate act, would ever have committed an unlawful act with a minor? No, we can not. Does the operation fit neatly into Jeanine Pirro's paradigm of self-promotion? Yes, it does.

While every citizen, particularly parents of young children, should want to see pedophiles apprehended and kept from inappropriate contact with minors, there are questions, however, which beg for answers:

Was it only a coincidence that Jeanine Pirro, who had been the District Attorney for nearly six years, suddenly started her sting operation in 1999, shortly after the tax fraud case became publicly known? After all, by her own admission, she was first introduced to the potential Internet problem back in 1994, in her very first year as D.A.. A postman from Seattle and a fourteen year old girl from Mamaroneck drew national attention when they were inadvertently discovered by the girl's mother at a mall in Westchester.

If she really was so concerned that such Internet contacts might pose a significant problem, why did it take her so long to respond? Jeanine claims that she personally campaigned in Albany "to persuade the state legislature to make typing dirty with a minor on the Internet into a felony." A research of the legislative history of S.210-E entitled "In Relation to Disseminating Indecent Materials to Minors, Through Any Computer Communication System," reveals the following:

The bill received final legislative passage on January 22, 1996, having received unanimous consent in the Senate, and near unanimous approval in the Assembly. Signed and approved by Governor Pataki on September 4, 1996, it became effective on November 1, 1996. Jeanine Pirro did not avail herself of the statute's provisions until her first sting arrest of Robert DeCarlo on July

21, 1999, fully 33 months later.

In three letters to the Governor, dated January 23, January 26, and July 11, 1996, State Senator William Sears, sponsor of the bill, made no mention of Jeanine whatsoever. A careful review of the "bill jacket" reveals that it was first introduced in the Senate on January 4, 1995. It required just nine months to reconcile the Senate and Assembly versions.

In all fairness to Jeanine, she did send a letter to Governor Pataki on February 13, 1996 urging his signature. The letter, of exactly 200 words, was one of several received, some urging passage and some calling for veto. The Civil Liberties Union and other organizations expressed concerns about possible constitutional violations.[30]

Most significant, from a credibility standpoint, was the last sentence of her letter. After alluding to a proposal of her own, she wrote, "However, in view of the legislative support for S.210-D, I urge you to sign it into law so that we may deter and adequately punish those who would seek to lure minors with sexually explicit computer communications."

If that was truly her intent, why did it take her nearly three years to do it? Despite all of her claims of having championed the legislation, she let it gather dust for 33 months until she needed some high-profile device, which could divert the public's attention from her and her husband's unlawful tax scheme.

Jeanine says of her Internet sting, "There is no question we have deterred many people from doing what they might otherwise do." But, that is a very questionable conclusion. While it is true, that over a two and a half year period, her operators have managed to lure and trap 50 adult males, there is no evidence, in the cases of 35 of them, that they ever previously had, or would ever have had, any inappropriate contact with a minor were it not for Jeanine's "crime creations."

Given what we know about true pedophiles, and the repetitive nature of their activities, there would appear to be two fundamental flaws in Pirro's justification argument. First, even if 15 of all those arrested might fit the behavior pattern of a pedophile, and might reasonably be expected to seek inappropriate contact with minors, the expenditure of resources over two and a half years would hardly seem justified. Second, given the fact that six out of seven of those convicted, plead to such minor offenses as to require no jail-time, where is the deterrent she claims?

Consider too; aside from the recent revelations about certain clergy, whose lifestyle of sexual deprivation sets them apart from the general population, where is the spate of pedophilic activity Jeanine Pirro claims to be shielding our children from? To be sure, there are pedophiles inside and outside of Westchester, who will target minors inside her jurisdiction. What proof have we that Jeanine's high-profile publicity generating operation achieves anything more? In fact, if her operation was truly a deterrent to such unlawful activity, one could reasonably expect a tapering off of the number of those snared in the sting as word of its existence has gotten around. However, such has not been the case.

With an operating budget of some 18 million dollars annually, not to mention the infusion of huge amounts of confiscated cash and other assets,[31] some 118 attorneys, and 34 investigators, at her disposal for more than eight years, one might expect "less sizzle, and more steak," to have come from Jeanine Pirro's office. The simple fact remains that she has been woefully short in many areas. Why else would she repeatedly seek to take credit for the accomplishments of others?

Her relationship with Carl Vergari, her mentor and former

employer, is a clear example of her total lack of humility, or honesty, and her incessant need to enhance her image. Carl's letter, dated February 27, 1997, and forwarded to Jeanine, with copies to the Gannett Newspapers and *The New Yorker magazine,* was provoked by a "puff-piece" in the magazine. The letter speaks volumes, and is reproduced in its entirety

No clearer example of Jeanine Pirro's manipulation of the truth to suit her momentary political agenda can be found in print than a comparison of two magazine puff articles published precisely five years apart. In the February 25, 1997 issue of *The New Yorker* magazine it was indicated that the enabling Internet legislation was passed, effective November 1996, supposedly as the result of Jeanine's "relentless lobbying efforts." Yet, in *New York* magazine published February 25, 2002, she would have us believe that the legislation was not passed and available until early 1999, just a few months prior to the start of her sting operation in July of that year.

Why the disparity? In the 1997 article, she was trying to take credit for passage of the law. However, in the article five years later, she was trying to avoid the truthful conclusion of many observers, that she started up the high-profile sting operation to divert attention from the tax fraud scandal.

As with most pathological liars, not only does Jeanine tell a lie repeatedly until she appears to believe it, but she is also willing to bring on a new story on a moment's notice to accommodate any contrary notion she might next want to float. I was personally reminded of her ability to manufacture a lie instantly when I greeted her at the Wedra trial.

As she approached the elevator, where I was standing, I greeted her and extended my hand, as I had often done. Refusing

Feb. 28, 1997 letter written by former Westchester County District Attorney Carl A. Vergari and sent to his successor, Jeanine Pirro:

Dear Jeanine.

Congratulations on your puff piece in The New Yorker. I marvel at your ability to get so much media coverage, and wonder how much of the People's time goes into this effort. But I digress.

I abhor fabrication of facts ‑ falsehoods made for the purpose of self-aggrandizement. I was annoyed at - but ignored - your claims as "founder" of the Domestic Violence Unit. I did not make an issue of it because I did not wish to create the appearance of controversy between us in your bids for election to County Court and District Attorney.

I accepted your tearful and emotional apologies for the "B-" you put on my performance as District Attorney - given "under pressure from the Gannett Editors." So much for courageous loyalty, particularly since I saved your political life during the fiasco of your bid for lieutenant governor.

But I am afraid your saying you "persuaded" me to apply for Domestic Violence funding to start up a unit is something of a last straw.

Let me refresh your recollection on this matter. For the last two years prior to the Domestic Violence funding, I was Chairman of The National District Attorneys Association Commission on Victim Witness Assistance, and chaired with federal funding the creation of the Victim Witness Units and Programs in six jurisdictions in the United States.

It was during my dealings with the LEAA (Law Enforcement Assistance Administration) officials that discussions concerning aid to special classes of victims were had. I outlined to the federal funders the various ways I believed the prosecutor's office could play a vital role in dealing with domestic violence and child abuse problems. I was invited by them to apply for a grant, which, of course, I received.

You knew nothing about this and played no role in this process. I convinced the DelBello administration to accept the grant. It was then that I called you in to tell you about it and to tell you that I was putting you in charge of the Unit.

As if it were yesterday, I recall your wide-eyed question, "What will we have to do?" I threw you a yellow pad and said, "Make a list," and defined the steps that we should take, including a Chiefs of Police conference which I called.

When the Unit was finally up, you took over and did a fine job. I personally saved the Unit when DelBello threatened to kill it by not providing County funds when the grant expired.

Jeanine, I am proud of my 26-year career as District Attorney and all of the programs which I instituted, including the Local Court Prosecutions, the Branch Office System, the Career Criminal Prosecution Unit, the Major Violence Offenders Program, the Victim Witness Assistance Unit, and the Domestic Violence/Child Abuse Unit. The entire organization which you now head and which administers Criminal Justice in Westchester, was created by me with the help of many other outstanding Assistants who, unfortunately, did not receive the public attention which you seem to attract.

I wish you well in the future, but will no longer silently tolerate outright distortions and falsehoods about my record.

Sincerely,

Carl A. Vergari
CAV: S
P.S. A copy of this letter is being sent to the Editors of The New Yorker and the Gannett Newspapers.

to shake it, she instantly concocted a story about my having refused to shake hers some months earlier, which was a total lie. What she didn't take the time to discover was that the fellow standing next to me was a *New York Post* reporter, intrigued by her infantile behavior.

Jeanine Pirro is not just any public office holder. She is the chief law enforcement officer of Westchester County, the ultimate arbiter of who will be prosecuted and who will not. Entrusted with such awesome power over the lives of nearly one million people, her demonstrated disregard for truth and human dignity renders her office a tyranny and a fraud. Only an individual motivated by a lust for power, and a hunger for material wealth, unrestrained by ethics or conscience, could turn the office into the device it has become.

Jeanine Pirro has occupied the office of District Attorney in the most aggressive sense of the word. Her regime has distorted and warped the normal function of a district attorney's office by essentially turning the legal authority, together with the human and financial resources at her disposal, into her personal possession, - a center-piece in the self-promoting organism that is the Jeanine Machine.

One need only speak with respected members of the Defense Bar to grasp the functional burden Jeanine's persona has imposed upon the criminal justice system in Westchester. She refuses to entrust ultimate decision making authority to anyone other than herself, irrespective of how serious or mundane a case may be. Her objective is always the same, to obtain a conviction, and thus enhance her record and public image.

To achieve her goal, she typically over-charges defendants, causing the plea-bargaining process to be unnecessarily extended, clogging calendars, and creating undue financial expenditure by defendants and the County alike. Her theory is to wear down defendants financially and emotionally, with costly court appearances, until she forces them into submission. She knows full well that, in most cases, defendants suffer the most with "justice delayed." Time lost from work, as well as costly legal representation, combine to soften up resistance. The prosecutor has little to lose in the 'delay equation.'

Under the 180.80 Rule of the Criminal Procedure Law a defendant charged in a felony-complaint, and incarcerated, is entitled to grand jury action within six days (144 hours) of arrest, or a felony hearing. Mere presentation to a grand jury does not, ordinarily, satisfy the rule. The grand jury must also act. In many jurisdictions, where a grand jury may not always be sitting, felony hearings are more frequently employed, as is the case in Westchester.

In neighboring Bronx County the 180.80 Rule is strictly enforced. In that County, there are always sitting grand juries available, and the D.A. prefers that option to felony hearings. Failure to bring about grand jury action within the required 144 hour limit will result in the release from custody of a defendant, even one charged with murder. By comparison with Bronx County, criminal defendants in Westchester are at a decided disadvantage. The D.A. holds many more cards. Her office is able to get away with many more acts of bad faith, particularly in preliminary proceedings, which often occur in justice courts.[32]

Given the rotating pool of Legal Aid attorneys, a system previously discussed, the circumstances clearly favor the prosecutor, particularly with indigent defendants. The imbalance is crucial, particularly in light of Jeanine's overarching objective. In short, the system in place in Westchester is ideally tailored to her warped perception of her role.

For all the edge she keeps for her office, morale amongst her staff, particularly her attorneys, is notoriously poor. Women account for only 40 out of 118 assistant district attorneys, and 29 of those 40 are stuck working at the lowest two levels of eight tiers. At last accounting, amongst 47 attorneys and investigators earning $100,000 or more, per year, only nine are women. A "glass ceiling" is never a happy work environment.

Jeanine is apparently the kind of woman who, once having climbed to the top of the ladder, is unwilling to permit other women to duplicate her feat. Amongst 34 criminal investigators, only two are women, raising questions about how the office manages certain sensitive interviews and investigations. Once, again the "gender warp," as with other aspects of the office, may be directly attributable to Jeanine's controlling personal agenda.

It is widely known that Jeanine 'plays favorites' with her staff. Those who become involved in her political campaigns, or assist with her or Al's personal problems, can count on choice assignments and higher wages. Some who come on board through relatives who have contributed to her campaign may start at a higher salary. Such was the case with ADA Richard Portale, whose prior arrest record was completely overlooked until he got into trouble with the law in a Florida motel. His uncle, publisher of *Elle* magazine was a substantial contributor to Jeanine's 1997 campaign.

Unfortunately, a significant number of her professional staff were hired by Jeanine, and have never known any other office. Of those who were hired by her predecessor, Carl Vergari, many are merely putting in their time to their pensions; going through the motions. Others who worked under Vergari, have gone into private practice or to other government agencies, rather than remain a part of her regime.

Unlike her last opponent, Tony Castro, and many of the highly regarded district attorneys in Westchester and the Metropolitan, New York area, Jeanine Pirro has shown little inclination to turn her assistant D.A.'s into the finest attorneys they can possibly become. On the contrary, competence in others can be quite threatening to her ego.

Tony Castro knew, that, had he won, one of the more challenging tasks he would have immediately faced would have been the retraining and reassignment of professional staff, in an effort to boost morale and normalize operations. It is no secret that many would have welcomed a new DA. Many have shared their distaste for the tension, the browbeating, and the profanity they must accept from Jeanine. Some have expressed disappointment with her lack of confidence in them to make important decisions and "think on their feet."

Restoring the District Attorney's Office

Tony Castro had a broad smile on his face when he told a table full of Jeanine's assistant district attorneys, which she had brought to the Hispanic Police Officers dinner, "I come not as a conqueror, but as a liberator." However, he could not have been more serious.

The next District Attorney of Westchester will need to be a person of patience and dedication, a professional prosecutor prepared to perform the job, properly and also to redirect and rebuild the organization. It will require someone willing to make a long-term commitment, because considerable time will be necessary merely to undo the damage left in Jeanine Pirro's wake. It will require someone willing, and able, to teach by example.

Re-education and re-deployment of staff in ways more consistent with the needs of citizens rather than the personal needs of the D.A. will go a long way to focus attention upon their legitimate mission. Not only must the "glass ceiling" be shattered, but affirmative employment programs, such as job-sharing, for family and personal leave, as well as equal opportunity advancement, and greater diversity, must be installed. Professional and support staff must sense that there is a real future in their employment. Loyalty based on mutual respect, rather than fear, must be developed.

Initiative and productivity, will be spawned as the staff recognizes the new outwardly focused emphasis of the office. Self-esteem and pride will be restored as the new D.A. demonstrates a willingness to share decision making, as well as credit for accomplishment. Honesty, integrity and accountability must govern every transaction.

It will be necessary to put the news media, particularly *The Journal News*, on notice that information coming from the District Attorney's Office will be factual and necessary public information, not public relations. The "right of the public to know" will not be distorted for purposes of self-promotion. Reporters will no longer need to write "puff articles" about the D.A. in order to be sure of getting genuine news releases.

The Westchester District Attorney's Office will, again, be recognized as a serious player in the world of law enforcement and criminal prosecution. Police agencies, in all 42 jurisdictions within the county, will know that they are free to perform their duties without being concerned about "making the D.A.. look good." Finally, the next D.A. will encourage cooperation and coordination of effort, and not "upstage" those in uniform.

Taking Back Westchester

Essentially, there are three means by which Jeanine Pirro is' likely to be relieved of her position, and each involves a separate time-table and different implications. Most probably, barring some unforeseeable event, Jeanine will serve out her present term, and be defeated by Tony Castro or another opponent, should Castro decide not to run. In that event, all of the issues involving her staff, will have been intensified by a full twelve years of her regime.

Another possible outcome might involve Jeanine's being appointed to another position. Such an outcome would necessitate the appointment of an interim D.A., and the holding of a special election. That could, of course, come at any time.

Finally, it is not impossible that a federal investigation into her culpable conduct, and/or her unconstitutional practices as D.A., or perhaps a successful Section 1983 action might force her from office. That too could come at any time. However, wishful thinking is not productive.

Jeanine, of course, would prefer elevation to a higher office, either state, or federal, for several reasons. It would get her off the 'hot seat' she has created for herself, while satisfying her ego. It would also avoid the certain defeat she would suffer at the hands of Tony Castro if she ran for a fourth term.

One can not contemplate the removal of Jeanine Pirro from the District Attorney's Office without also contemplating the collapse of The Cabal and the Jeanine Machine, liberating the political infrastructure of Westchester. Without the power to prosecute, to harass, and intimidate, her "reign of terror," would screech to a halt.

If, as proclaimed by William Pitt, "Where law ends, tyranny begins," conversely, we may reasonably expect that where law is restored, tyranny will end. Thus, the removal of Jeanine Pirro from the District Attorney's Office, by whatever lawful means, at whatever moment, will bring a new and brighter day to the people of Westchester County.

END NOTES

[1] Substantial evidence connecting Jeanine to the tax fraud conspiracy was presented at the trial of her husband, Albert Pirro in Federal District Court, White Plains, New York, in June 2000.

[2] The program provided subsidized decent housing for formerly homeless, mildly retarded adults.

[3] It is generally known that each time an inmate transfers to a new prison population he is tested, and often forced to "get married" by fellow prisoners.

[4] New York State Code of Criminal Procedure requirement.

[5] Lee was under no pressure from his employer. He was uncomfortable owing money to anyone, and had set up a repayment schedule that was too ambitious.

[6] A defendant can not legally be compelled to waive such rights. ADA Scharf's action was indicative of the arrogance and distortion of judicial process so commonplace under Jeanine Pirro.

[7] It is unlawful for a prosecutor to withhold exculpatory information from a defendant.

[8] The government accepted the payment but took the position that the amended returns and payment constituted a confession of guilt.

[9] Although tax fraud was clearly an element of the Hudson Valley Hospital swindle — bribery, kickback conspiracy, and fiduciary breach were the primary offences committed.

[10] Jeanine Pirro intentionally disregarded the gag order of Texas District Court Judge Susan Criss in the homicide prosecution of Robert Durst for the murder of his neighbor in Galveston. She claimed that she was immune from the order.

[11] The information was the basis of Tony Castro's first press release, August 22, 2001, revealing the "glass ceiling" in Jeanine's office.

[12] Restiano, a Republican, intends to run for Mayor of Yonkers when Spencer's term expires. Toward that end, it has been revealed that she contributed $36,000 to help fund the campaign to keep term limits, under which Mayor Spencer is barred from seeking a third term. She was named, together with State Senator Nick Spano, in connection with illegal telephone messages in support of term limits uncovered by the Yonkers Police Department. District Attorney Pirro refused to investigate the charges.

[13] Philip Werbel pleaded guilty to Tampering With A Primary Election, as a misdemeanor, and was sentenced on April 22, 2002 to three years probation and a $1,000 fine. Anthony Mangone did not plead guilty to any wrongdoing, and remains a part-time employee of State Senator Nick Spano earning $50,000 while employed full-time by a law firm connected with Al Pirro in a building owned by Al Pirro.

[14] The combatants were mostly Italian-American and Albanian-American males in their twenties and thirties. There had been tension between them for a long time.

[15] Lisa Copeland, City Clerk of Mount Vernon, was not required to resign her position in order to run for County Clerk. She frequently joined Tony Castro on the campaign trail.

[16] There are clubs in Yonkers, New Rochelle, Mount Vernon, Ossining, and Tarrytown. Fundraising events were held at each.

[17] An inexperienced volunteer using a preprinted mailing list of labels of members of the Westchester Women's Bar Association, had inadvertently forwarded an invitation to a fundraiser for Tony Castro to Jeanine Pirro at her office. Jeanine deliberately uses her office address instead of her home address thereby causing **all** such correspondence to be delivered to her office. Missing the humor in the mistake, Jeanine went to *The Journal News* charging Castro with a violation for having solicited a public official for political purposes. Her citation of the statute was totally incorrect.

[18] The 'white paper' was actually a document of some 150 pages containing material from the original 67-count federal indictment as well as transcripts from the tax fraud trial.

[19] In her anger Jeanine attempted to turn individuals and organizations associated with Polly against her. She tried to keep them from attending Polly's testimonial retirement dinner.

[20] One of many instances of *The Journal News* working for the re-election of Jeanine Pirro.

[21] Dennis Alvarez-Hernandez, charged in the killing of his girlfriend Patricia Torres and two of her children in Yonkers in September 2000.

[22] Excuse number one.

[23] Excuse number two.

[24] Excuse number three.

[25] Excuse number four.

[26] Reprinted on pages 151 and 152

[27] In February 2002, two reporters for *The Journal News* revealed that the "white paper" received from Tony Castro had vanished.

[28] Under the circumstances, conduct well within the legally permissible "Defense of Others" as a justifiable homicide.

[29] We knew throughout the campaign that Jeanine Pirro and Andy Spano were conducting polls, the results of which were not made public. As time went on it became clear that Jeanine was becoming increasingly concerned, based upon the desperation of her activities. In the closing weeks of the campaign she engaged in clearly unlawful activity including personal visits to merchants to tear down Castro signs and erect her own.

[30] Some of those same constitutional issues involving Freedom of Speech were addressed by the United States Supreme Court in April 2002 when they struck down certain criminal statutes intended to prohibit "simulated adolescent and child sexual activity."

[31] In a case some years ago Jeanine Pirro went after Herve Filion, most winning driver in harness racing history, who was also an addicted gambler. He was charged, together with notorious bookmaker Danny Kramer of Scarsdale, in connection with a race fixing conspiracy. Kramer was clearly the real villain in the case, having corrupted several drivers in the past.

Herve's brilliant career was ended, but Danny Kramer walked because Jeanine confiscated more than two million dollars cash gambling receipts from Kramer's home

[32] There are 42 separate jurisdictions in Westchester County. Many cases are first heard in town or village courts where defendants are brought before local justices who are not required to hold a law degree.

SUBJECT INDEX